VMware vRealize Operations Essentials

Harness the power of VMware vRealize Operations
to efficiently manage your IT infrastructure

Matthew Steiner

[PACKT] enterprise
PUBLISHING

professional expertise distilled

BIRMINGHAM - MUMBAI

VMware vRealize Operations Essentials

Copyright © 2015 Packt Publishing

First published: December 2015

Production reference: 1211215

Published by Packt Publishing Ltd.
Livery Place
35 Livery Street
Birmingham B3 2PB, UK.

ISBN 978-1-78528-475-5

www.packtpub.com

Credits

Author
Matthew Steiner

Reviewers
James Bowling

Rebecca Fitzhugh

Brian Ragazzi

Commissioning Editor
Ashwin Nair

Acquisition Editor
Shaon Basu

Content Development Editor
Dharmesh Parmar

Technical Editor
Namrata Patil

Copy Editors
Tani Kothari

Merilyn Pereira

Project Coordinator
Nikhil Nair

Proofreader
Safis Editing

Indexer
Rekha Nair

Graphics
Jason Monteiro

Production Coordinator
Aparna Bhagat

Cover Work
Aparna Bhagat

Foreword

Automators – the future kingmakers

Scale.

The future is always about scale—bigger, faster, and stronger.

As we sit here in a time when, once again, both application and infrastructure architectures are shifting, a trend emerges, and this time it is automation. IT has always been about building bigger; something I continually talk to customers about is how they need to look backwards to look forwards. Look at what you were doing 5 years ago in IT; it is very different from now. Now, you are doing more: managing more machines, supporting more applications, embracing more technologies, developing more business models, and simply put—more. Look 5 years ahead from now and there is even more.

However, you only have one pair of hands. So the answer is automation. Each growth phase in architecture drives you to abstract yourself up one layer and find ways of simplifying to stay ahead. Skills that used to be valuable, such as racking servers and plugging them in (where I started!), become commoditized. Now, building and managing individual VMs is also becoming an activity that is undifferentiated as architectures move to microservices and scale-out decoupled layers instead of the classic tightly coupled stacks.

The future kingmakers are those who can build those layers, automate them to within an inch of their lives and communicate through APIs.

The future belongs to those that can say to applications' teams, "I've got an API for that."

As someone who has picked up this book, you have already realized that, and are taking the right steps and are building your own future.

Enjoy.

Joe Baguley
VP & Chief Technology Officer
VMware EMEA

About the Author

Matthew Steiner is an experienced presales consultant with a career stretching back over 25 years in the IT industry, the last 16 years of which have been spent providing presales support for technology vendors.

He started his career as a PC engineer in the North East of England and then spent 7 years providing technical support and working on IT projects for The Royal Bank of Scotland.

In 2000, he moved into presales, first with Compaq and then HP and IBM, working with both x86 and UNIX architectures before moving into the software industry with VMware. He is currently a Lead Systems Engineer (SE) at VMware and has spent the last 3 years as a Cloud Management Platform Specialist SE. His focus is on vRealize Operations for which he is the presales lead in the UK.

Apart from the 'day job', providing technical sales support, Matthew is a regular contributor and speaker at events and conferences such as VMworld and local VMware User Groups (VMUGs), and is VMware's technical sponsor for the Scottish VMUG.

This is Matthew's first book, although he has also authored two Hands on Labs for VMware as well as white papers and other training materials throughout his career. He also maintains a blog at SEinTheCloud.wordpress.com, where he writes about his experiences as a presales consultant and the technologies he is working with.

Thank you to Jayne for putting up with me spending many evenings and weekends writing, and thank you to our cats, Lizzie and Smithy, for distracting me at times and standing on my keyboard!

Also, thank you to all my colleagues who helped me with ideas and support, particularly Peter Von Oven, who initially inspired me to write, and has mentored me through the process. Thanks also to the VMware OneCloud and Hands on Labs teams, without those environments I could not have written this book.

About the Reviewers

Rebecca Fitzhugh is an independent VMware consultant and VMware Certified Instructor whose primary focus is on architecting vSphere, vRealize, and Horizon infrastructures. She is a VMware vExpert and has obtained multiple levels of certification (VCP/VCAP), acquiring nearly 10 years of experience. Prior to becoming an instructor and consultant, Rebecca served 5 years in the United States Marine Corps where she assisted in the build-out and administration of multiple enterprise networks residing on virtual infrastructure. Her book, *vSphere Virtual Machine Management*, was published by Packt Publishing. You can follow her on Twitter at @rebeccafitzhugh.

Brian Ragazzi has been in the IT industry for more than 15 years, with experience of a wide variety of hardware, application delivery, data center virtualization, application development, cloud advisory services, and software engineering. He holds several certifications from Citrix, EMC, Microsoft, and VMware.

Brian has reviewed and contributed to *VMware vRealize Orchestrator Cookbook* as well as numerous white papers and solution guides.

He is a Cloud Solutions Consulting engineer at EMC, currently working with the EMC Federation Enterprise Hybrid Cloud solution, and specializes in Software Defined Data Center, IT automation, and day-2 operations.

Brian can be found online at http://brianragazzi.com or on Twitter @BrianPRagazzi.

www.PacktPub.com

Support files, eBooks, discount offers, and more

For support files and downloads related to your book, please visit www.PacktPub.com.

Did you know that Packt offers eBook versions of every book published, with PDF and ePub files available? You can upgrade to the eBook version at www.PacktPub.com and as a print book customer, you are entitled to a discount on the eBook copy. Get in touch with us at service@packtpub.com for more details.

At www.PacktPub.com, you can also read a collection of free technical articles, sign up for a range of free newsletters and receive exclusive discounts and offers on Packt books and eBooks.

https://www2.packtpub.com/books/subscription/packtlib

Do you need instant solutions to your IT questions? PacktLib is Packt's online digital book library. Here, you can search, access, and read Packt's entire library of books.

Why subscribe?

- Fully searchable across every book published by Packt
- Copy and paste, print, and bookmark content
- On demand and accessible via a web browser

Free access for Packt account holders

If you have an account with Packt at www.PacktPub.com, you can use this to access PacktLib today and view 9 entirely free books. Simply use your login credentials for immediate access.

Instant updates on new Packt books

Get notified! Find out when new books are published by following @PacktEnterprise on Twitter or the *Packt Enterprise* Facebook page.

Table of Contents

Preface

At VMware, we often talk about our clients' experiences with our technologies as journeys that they undertake.

The original journey was all about Virtualization; people started with virtualization first in their IT Department trying this magical new technology, before using it in Testing and Development and then in Production. The final step of their journey was to virtualize everything, including the most critical applications on which their business runs.

Now we are on a new journey, this time, to the Cloud. There are many different definitions of 'Cloud', but they share some common characteristics, such as:

- Pooling: This is the pooling of hardware resources so they can be shared as needed

- Elasticity: Leveraging the pooled resources to allow workloads to grow and shrink to meet demand as required in real time

- Automation: Everything in the cloud should be automated and fast; there should be no more waiting for administrators to spin up workloads or install applications

- Self Service: Consumers of cloud technology should be able to request the resources they want via a self-service portal or an API

Regardless of whether you are operating a private, public, or a hybrid cloud, you can expect to see these characteristics in place.

The technology that delivers on these cloud promises is a Cloud Management Platform (CMP), and VMware's CMP has three elements:

- vRealize Operations: This is a solution delivering on the operational disciplines required to operate your cloud.
- vRealize Automation: This has the capability to automate the creation and deletion of objects and workloads during their lifecycle in your cloud. This also includes a self-service portal and an API as well as governance in the form of approvals.
- vRealize Business: This provides visibility into the costs of running the workloads and services in your cloud.

This book is about the vRealize Operations part of VMware's CMP and will take you on a journey to understand how vRealize Operations can be used to deliver the operational disciplines demanded of today's cloud administrators.

What this book covers

Chapter 1, Introduction to vRealize Operations Manager, introduces the reader to vRealize Operations, providing an overview of its capabilities and architecture. Packaging and licensing will also be looked at in this chapter.

Chapter 2, Install, Configure, and Administer vRealize Operations Manager, starts by describing the planning, sizing, and design steps to be undertaken before deploying vRealize Operations Manager. We then go through the process of installing and configuring the solution and look at some of the administrative tasks and requirements.

Chapter 3, Dashboards, Badges, and Widgets, goes through the various elements in the vRealize Operations UI. We will look at the badges that are integral to the dashboards and then the out-of-the-box dashboards themselves. Finally, we will look at custom dashboards and the widgets that they are composed of.

Chapter 4, Views and Reports, examines the reporting capability of vRealize Operations. First, we will look at Views, including how to use the workspace to create your own custom views. Next, we will cover how these views can be combined to create reports that can be exported for external consumption.

Chapter 5, Alerts, Symptoms, Recommendations, and Actions, looks at the alerting framework within vRealize Operations and how content is provided in the form of alerts, symptoms, recommendations, and actions. We will also see how you can create custom alerting content yourself.

Chapter 6, Capacity Planning and Capacity Projects, examines the operational discipline of capacity planning. First, we will look at the capacity models that you can adopt. Next, we will look at capacity badges and dashboards, and finally, at how you can use the Capacity Projects feature to add future workloads to your capacity plans.

Chapter 7, vRealize Operations Manager Solutions, shows how you can extend the capabilities of vRealize Operations by adding Management Packs to manage other parts of your infrastructure. We will look at what is in Management Packs and how they are installed and used. Finally in this chapter, we will look at how you can keep your vRealize Operations solution up to date.

Chapter 8, vRealize Infrastructure Navigator, looks at how you can add visibility of application dependencies to your vRealize Operations implementation. We will go through the installation and configuration of the solution, see how it integrates with vRealize Operations, and how you can group interconnected VMs together.

Chapter 9, vRealize Log Insight Integration, examines how you can add further capability by implementing and integrating vRealize Log Insight. After looking at how you size and plan its deployment, we will show you how the solution is implemented and how it can be easily extended with Content Packs. We will also look at how Log Insight agents can capture additional logs from sources such as Windows Events.

Chapter 10, End Point Operations, covers how you can manage your Operating Systems and Applications through the installation of End Point Operations agents. We will look at the architecture and deployment of End Point Operations and the additional content that it provides.

What you need for this book

General knowledge of operating, managing, and troubleshooting the vSphere platform is essential in order to get the most out of this book. If you are a vSphere administrator, vRealize Operations will be a valuable tool to help you in your day-to-day job and this book will show you how.

The book has a lot of practical exercises in it, taking you through installation and configuration of the various components in the vRealize Operations solution. A home lab or test/development environment would be a good place to start; however, you will find that deploying the solution against a real environment with real workloads running will offer you the best experience.

You will need the following VMware software to work through all the exercises and examples in the book:

- vSphere 4.0 U2 or above (full integration with vRealize Operations requires vSphere 5.5 or above)

- vRealize Operations 6.1

- vRealize Log Insight 3.0

You can download 60 day evaluations of all this software from `my.vmware.com`.

Who this book is for

If you are a vSphere Administrator and are looking to deploy and use the vRealize Operations solution, this book is the ideal place to start. It will take you through implementing and using the entire solution, including vRealize Operations Manager, vRealize Log Insight, vRealize Infrastructure Navigator, and End Point Operations.

The exercises will also introduce you to customizing the solution to meet your own needs; you will soon be building your own dashboards and creating your own content using the alerting framework.

Conventions

In this book, you will find a number of text styles that distinguish between different kinds of information. Here are some examples of these styles and an explanation of their meaning.

Code words in text, database table names, folder names, filenames, file extensions, pathnames, dummy URLs, user input, and Twitter handles are shown as follows: "Enter the **FQDN**, **Username,** and **Password** for your vRealize Operations instance. Click on **Test Connection** to ensure the details are entered correctly."

New terms and **important words** are shown in bold. Words that you see on the screen, for example, in menus or dialog boxes, appear in the text like this: "To access the dashboards, navigate to **Home** and, in the **Dashboard List**, select **vSphere Dashboards**."

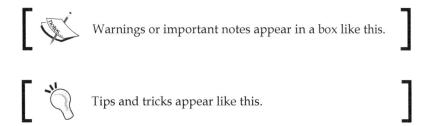

Warnings or important notes appear in a box like this.

Tips and tricks appear like this.

Reader feedback

Feedback from our readers is always welcome. Let us know what you think about this book—what you liked or disliked. Reader feedback is important for us as it helps us develop titles that you will really get the most out of.

To send us general feedback, simply e-mail `feedback@packtpub.com`, and mention the book's title in the subject of your message.

If there is a topic that you have expertise in and you are interested in either writing or contributing to a book, see our author guide at `www.packtpub.com/authors`.

Customer support

Now that you are the proud owner of a Packt book, we have a number of things to help you to get the most from your purchase.

Downloading the color images of this book

We also provide you with a PDF file that has color images of the screenshots/ diagrams used in this book. The color images will help you better understand the changes in the output. You can download this file from `https://www.packtpub.com/sites/default/files/downloads/VMwarevRealizeOperationsEssentials_ColorImages.pdf`.

Errata

Although we have taken every care to ensure the accuracy of our content, mistakes do happen. If you find a mistake in one of our books—maybe a mistake in the text or the code—we would be grateful if you could report this to us. By doing so, you can save other readers from frustration and help us improve subsequent versions of this book. If you find any errata, please report them by visiting http://www.packtpub.com/submit-errata, selecting your book, clicking on the **Errata Submission Form** link, and entering the details of your errata. Once your errata are verified, your submission will be accepted and the errata will be uploaded to our website or added to any list of existing errata under the Errata section of that title.

To view the previously submitted errata, go to https://www.packtpub.com/books/content/support and enter the name of the book in the search field. The required information will appear under the **Errata** section.

Piracy

Piracy of copyrighted material on the Internet is an ongoing problem across all media. At Packt, we take the protection of our copyright and licenses very seriously. If you come across any illegal copies of our works in any form on the Internet, please provide us with the location address or website name immediately so that we can pursue a remedy.

Please contact us at copyright@packtpub.com with a link to the suspected pirated material.

We appreciate your help in protecting our authors and our ability to bring you valuable content.

Questions

If you have a problem with any aspect of this book, you can contact us at questions@packtpub.com, and we will do our best to address the problem.

1
Introduction to vRealize Operations Manager

This first chapter introduces the reader to vRealize Operations Manager, starting with an overview of the solution, and how it fits into the rest of the VMware vRealize family of products.

The topics to be covered in this chapter include:

- Operational disciplines addressed by the solution, including performance management and capacity planning
- Solution architecture, addressing the needs of scalability and resilience
- Product packaging and licensing

A look at vRealize Operations Manager

vRealize Operations Manager is the core component of **vRealize Operations**, which itself is a suite of integrated products that provide intelligent operational capabilities for IT departments. The solution has been built, not just to monitor and manage vSphere, but also various pieces of infrastructure, such as storage, other hypervisors, operating systems, and applications.

The components that make up vRealize Operations are:

- vRealize Operations Manager
- vRealize Hyperic and End Point Operations
- vRealize Infrastructure Navigator
- vRealize Configuration Manager

Other solutions within the vRealize family of products that integrate tightly with vRealize Operations are:

- vRealize Log Insight
- vRealize Business Standard
- vRealize Automation

The main focus of this book is the vRealize Operations Manager component of vRealize Operations. However, we will look at **vRealize Log Insight** integration in *Chapter 9, vRealize Log Insight Integration* and at **End Point Operations** in *Chapter 10, End Point Operations*.

Integrations with the other components of the vRealize portfolio, or with other hardware such as EMC, Dell, or Hitachi storage arrays, are provided by **Management Packs**. Management Packs and VMware's Solution Exchange will be covered in *Chapter 7, vRealize Operations Manager Solutions*.

Operational disciplines addressed by vRealize Operations

As the name of the solution suggests, vRealize Operations is an operational management solution. It has been designed to address the operational disciplines of **Performance**, **Capacity**, **Configuration**, and **Compliance**.

Each of these can be thought of as being related and acting in concert with each other. Together they define the level of **availability** achieved by the infrastructure being managed, and whether the **Service Level Agreements** (**SLAs**) in place between the business and the IT department are being met.

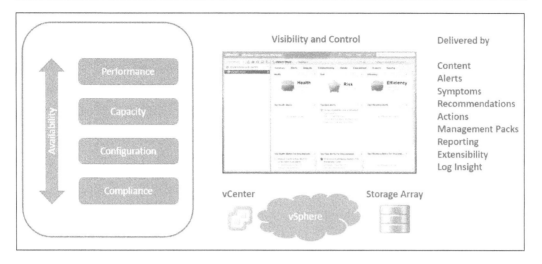

For example, if there is insufficient capacity in a cluster, the performance of VMs in that cluster may deteriorate, and the service or application that these VMs support may become unavailable.

vRealize Operations uses a variety of features such as content, alerts, symptoms, management packs, and reporting to provide the required visibility and control of the infrastructure, and deliver on these operational disciplines. Let's look at them in more detail.

Performance

vRealize Operations Manager monitors the performance of managed systems, and provides the system administrators with a set of very intuitive dashboards that provide them quick visualization of problems and issues that may arise. When the performance of the systems is not as expected, the solution helps with troubleshooting by directing the administrator quickly to the root cause of the problem. This is all underpinned with **analytics** and **content**.

Analytics

Every five minutes, vRealize Operations collects and stores the **metric** and **property** data about every resource it manages. The data is kept for six months at full granularity and is used by the Analytics engine to allow the system to understand normal behavior.

The frequency of data collection and retention is tunable from the default 5 minute data collection and 6 months data retention periods. However, care must be taken when changing these as they can affect, quite significantly, the sizing requirements of the vRealize Operations nodes.

Every night, a set of analytics algorithms are run against every metric's historical dataset, to determine the expected behavior of each metric for the upcoming 24 hours. This expected behavior for a metric is called a **Dynamic Threshold (DT)**. As metrics are collected and stored, they are compared against the DT to determine whether the object is exhibiting normal behavior. This is described in more detail in *Figure 1.1*.

The analytics are designed to look for different patterns of behavior, such as hourly, daily, weekly, monthly, and quarterly.

It will obviously take some time for vRealize Operations to learn all the expected behavior, as it needs to observe at least three data points to start seeing a trend, and many more to predict the trend with greater confidence. For example, a metric exhibiting a weekly cadence of behavior requires at least three weeks of data for a weekly trend to be detected.

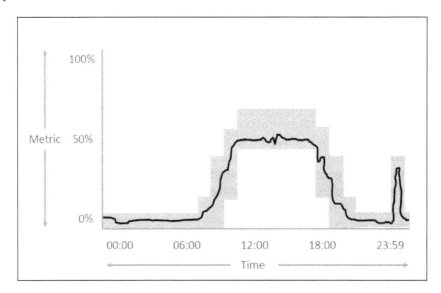

Figure 1.1

The preceding simplified example shows how a DT and metric may be measured and tracked. The grey shading is the DT, and the diagram shows that during the early morning it is expecting this metric's value to be 0-10%, then 50-60% during the work day, and then back down to 0-10% for the evening. There is a short peak just before midnight, which is possibly a batch or a backup job. The black line is the observed metric and we can see that normal behavior has occurred; so in this case, there is no alerting to be done as the metric is operating normally.

If an observed metric deviates outside of the DT range, it is classed as an **Anomaly** and highlighted in yellow in the **Metric Selectors** and the associated **Metric Graphs** in the vRealize Operations dashboards.

The number of anomalies observed over time is also recorded for every object, and vRealize Operations uses these **derived metrics** to determine whether the number of anomalies being observed is significant and if it is required that an alert is generated.

Performance or availability problems are generally caused by something different happening with the resources within an environment, and this "something different" causes associated metrics to breach their DTs. This means that the majority of alerts that are performance or metric related will only be generated when abnormal behavior occurs. This dramatically reduces the number of alerts that IT operations receive and increases the quality of those alerts.

Content

The content baked into vRealize Operations is how the solution creates the intelligent and meaningful *alerts*. There is a lot of content provided by the solution and much more content will be added with the installation of Management Packs. Custom content can also be created very easily and will be described in *Chapter 5*, *Alerts, Symptoms, Recommendations, and Actions*.

An example of one of the *out of the box* content alerts and how it is constructed is as follows:

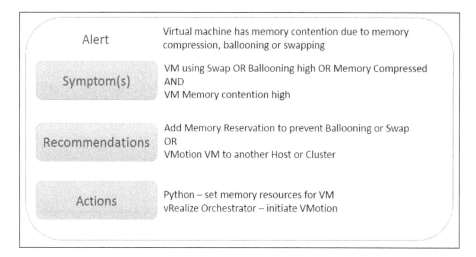

- **Symptom(s)**: They are descriptions of one or more conditions under which the alert is triggered. In the preceding example, the symptoms are that a VM is swapping to disk, has high ballooning or has memory compressed, and has high memory contention.

- **Recommendations**: They are remediation action(s) that can be taken to resolve the symptoms. In the preceding case, the action may be to add a memory reservation or initiate a vMotion to migrate some VMs to another host or cluster with more capacity.

- **Actions**: They act on the recommendation(s). vRealize Operations has the capability to initiate actions using Python scripts or vRealize Orchestrator workflows to carry out the recommendations. In the preceding example, the *out of the box* Python script can be used to set a memory reservation, or vRealize Orchestrator can be used to initiate a vMotion.

Dynamic thresholds and hard thresholds

Alerting based on metrics, which are outside the range of the calculated DTs, can be considered fairly generic and caused by "things happening differently". They tend to be used to troubleshoot and alert on unexpected behavior.

As well as triggering alerts based on *unexpected* behavior, much of the content in vRealize Operations Manager is based on *specific* behavior and documented best practices. For instance, storage latency would generally be considered performance impacting by a storage administrator, when it reaches 20-30ms.

Content within vRealize Operations Manager can also include **Hard Thresholds (HTs)**, such as a figure of 20-30ms for storage latency, which can trigger alerts regardless of the state of the DT for the given metrics.

Content and alerts will be covered in much more depth in *Chapter 5, Alerts, Symptoms, Recommendations, and Actions*.

Capacity

Capacity management is one of the most important disciplines in IT Operations. Unfortunately, as virtualization has matured, traditional capacity management techniques have tended not to keep up with the technology. My experience of working with clients with mature virtualized environments and outdated capacity management practices is that they find themselves with a lot of underutilized infrastructure, resulting in a lot of wasted resources.

vRealize Operations Manager has a very rich capacity engine, which will help with this, illustrating capacity utilization in two main ways:

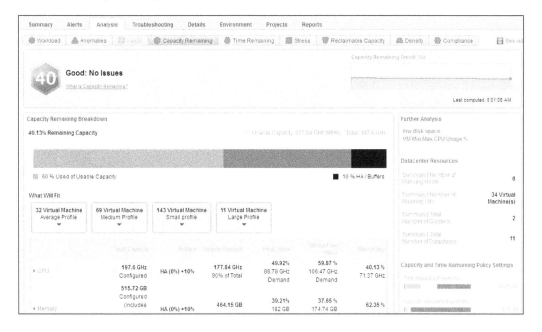

- **Capacity remaining**: Taking into account the reserved capacity for vSphere HA and the headroom buffers, it answers the question about *how much capacity remaining does a given resource have?*. In the preceding screenshot, we can see that we have enough capacity available in this resource to support a further 32 average sized virtual machines.

- **Time remaining**: Again, taking into account the reserved capacity for vSphere HA and the headroom buffers, it answers the question *when am I going to run out of capacity?*. In the following screenshot, we can see that the capacity for this resource is going to run out in 87 days and that CPU is the constrained resource.

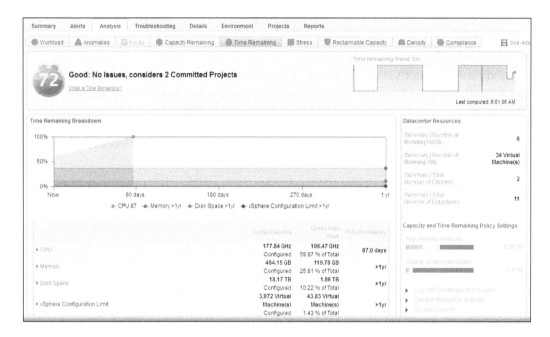

Capacity models

Every object or resource in vRealize Operations can have a capacity model configured against it. This describes the metric(s) used to determine the capacity and the other factors, or constraints to be considered, such as vSphere HA. The models themselves are not configurable, however, *how* they are applied generally is configurable, and is managed within the policies section of vRealize Operations.

 Many of the VMware and third-party Management Packs have capacity models associated with the resources they are managing. The documentation for these Management Packs usually provides the administrator detail on how the capacity of a given object type is calculated.

The policies governing the capacity management in vRealize Operations are very granular and controllable. This allows the administrator to define what combination of demand or allocation capacity policies are applied against specific resources or groups of resources. This will be covered in detail in *Chapter 6, Capacity Planning and Capacity Projects*.

Capacity projects

As well as understanding the current capacity and the time remaining, many organizations will have ongoing projects that are going to add planned workload or additional hardware to their infrastructure. A new feature, **Capacity Projects**, introduced in vRealize Operations 6.0, allows the administrator to define these forecasted changes in the workload or resources, and assign a date against them.

The effect on capacity and the time remaining can then be visualized and any capacity shortfalls identified. The projects can be subsequently committed and they will then be reflected in the real-time capacity reporting.

For example, if an infrastructure has the capacity for a further 50 average sized VMs, but a project is planned to implement 20 average sized VMs, the capacity dashboards, badges, and reports will all change to reflect that there is now only capacity for 30 average sized VMs.

Configuration and compliance

The final operational disciplines being addressed are **configuration** and **compliance**. Misconfiguration of systems is the root cause of a large proportion of system outages; so ensuring that all your systems are configured the way you want them to be is one of the key weapons in ensuring up-time.

As well as ensuring up-time, there may be **legal and regulatory** reasons, such as PCI-DSS, for the systems to be configured in a certain way. Alternatively, there may be security or hardening standards that an organization's security department determines are essential, to ensure that the integrity of the systems is maintained. Both of these would be classed as compliance requirements.

For in-depth configuration and compliance, vCenter Configuration Manager is provided as part of vRealize Operations Advanced and Enterprise editions. However, the use of vCenter Configuration Manager is not covered in this book.

With the release of vRealize Operations 6.0, some configuration and compliance capabilities have been introduced into the vRealize Operations Manager platform. As well as collecting metrics, vRealize Operations now collects **properties** from the ESXi hosts and the VM containers.

These properties can be used to assess the configuration posture of the ESXi hosts and the VM containers, using the Alerts, Symptoms, Recommendations, and Actions framework.

Content has been created that reflects the vSphere Hardening Guidelines, which means that, out of the box, vRealize Operations can now report on how compliant the ESXi hosts and the VM containers are against these guidelines. The reporting is available through the alerts, views, and reports functionality, and also via the **Compliance badge** in the vRealize Operations dashboards.

vSphere Hardening Guidelines will be covered in *Chapter 5, Alerts, Symptoms, Recommendations, and Actions.*

Architecture, scalability, and resilience

Like most solutions from VMware, vRealize Operations Manager is delivered as a virtual appliance based on SUSE Linux.

 vRealize Operations Manager can also be installed on Windows or Linux. However, that needs special consideration, so is outside the scope of this book.

Appliance nodes and components

The basic building block of vRealize Operations is the virtual appliance **node**. The solution can be scaled from a single node to a maximum of 16 nodes, to support larger scale deployments or **high availability (HA)**. Remote collector nodes can also be additionally installed to collect the metric data from remote datacenters with limited bandwidth connectivity.

Regardless of the role of a node, the same OVF is used to deploy the virtual appliance, and, as of vRealize Operations Manager 6.0, there is no longer the requirement to host remote collectors on Linux or Windows.

To a great extent, this has made the design, implementation, and management of vRealize Operations very straightforward, relative to the complexity and capabilities the solution provides.

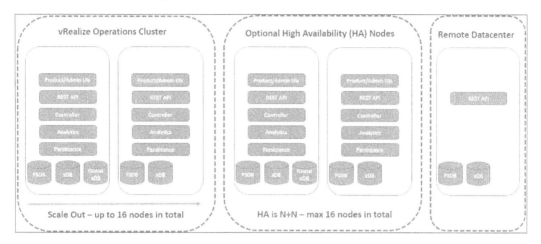

The preceding diagram shows the different roles the nodes can take. Although they are all installed using the same virtual appliance OVA file and contain the same code, the nodes will only run the services required to fulfill their role. The roles are as follows:

- **Master Node**: The first node you install in the cluster. This is the controlling node for the cluster.
- **Data Node**: This adds additional scale to the cluster. Multiple data nodes are deployed under the following circumstances:
    - If the scalability limits of a single large node is reached.
    - When a larger number of smaller nodes is desired. For example, the ESXi hosts for the nodes may not be able to support the size of the VM required by a large node.
- **Master Replica Node**: This is a copy of the Master Node, containing the Global xDB, and it will take over the operation of the cluster if the Master Node fails.

- **Remote Collector Node**: This resides in a remote datacenter to collect the metrics and properties from a remote vCenter. This is used under the following circumstances:
  - When bandwidth to the remote datacenter is limited. A Remote Collector Node reduces the bandwidth requirements by approximately 65%.
  - If a firewall is in place between the Master Node and the vCenter server, and the appropriate ports cannot be opened.

The components running within the nodes are as follows:

- **Product and Admin User Interface**: The Product UI is the main UI used to access vRealize Operations and is available on all the nodes except for Remote Collectors. The Admin UI is used for cluster administration and is available on all the nodes.

- **REST API**: A pluggable service used by the vRealize Operations adapters to collect data and metrics. The API also allows the external services to interface with vRealize Operations.

- **Controller**: It ensures insertion of the collected data to the correct resources, and retrieves the data queries when requested. It also ensures consistency of the data across all the nodes.

- **Analytics**: The analytics engine performs metric calculation when the metrics are ingested, and runs the nightly Dynamic Threshold jobs. Analytics is also responsible for triggering alerts.

- **Persistence**: Every node persists its own set of data to the local disk for processing.

- **FSDB**: It is the data store for metric data.

- **xDB**: It stores the alerts and the alarm data, as well as the **Historical Inventory Service** (**HIS**), which is responsible for storing the resource properties and relationships.

- **Global xDB**: It contains the cluster configuration data.

Architecture

Once a vRealize Operations cluster is established, **solutions** are configured to connect the cluster to the infrastructure to be managed, as can be seen in the following diagram.

The first solution to be configured will be to one or more vSphere environments, connecting the built in adapter to the vCenter Server(s) supporting those environments.

Extending the solution to provide performance and health monitoring, and the capacity planning for storage is enabled, either by using the generic vRealize Operations Management Pack for Storage Devices, or one of the specific Management Packs from the storage vendor or third party developers. More information on these integrations can be found in *Chapter 7, vRealize Operations Manager Solutions*.

Management Packs written by VMware are included with editions of vRealize Operations, depending on the edition licensed. Management packs written by third parties are provided and supported by the third party and may require an additional license fee.

If vCloud Air or Amazon EC2 are used, Management Packs are available to connect the solution to these environments.

Integration with the other vRealize components, such as vRealize Hyperic or End Point Operations and vRealize Log Insight is also enabled using the Management Packs.

Finally, if there are remote datacenters, remote collector nodes can be configured to collect the metrics if low bandwidth conditions exist.

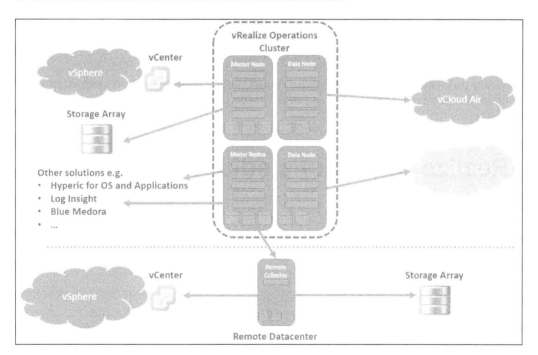

Scalability

One of the design goals of vRealize Operations was to meet the scalability requirements of the largest infrastructures, which can run to tens of thousands of VMs and other resources.

Every 5 minutes, vRealize collects and stores about 250 metrics per VM, 500 metrics per host, and, typically, 50 or more metrics for the other object types. As a result, the total quantity of stored data, and the volume of the metrics being analyzed every night, can become significant.

 An environment with 1,000 VMs will typically have over 300,000 metrics being collected every 5 minutes and analyzed every night. With the default 6 month data retention period and HA in place, that means over 30 billion data points being stored!

VMware provides detailed sizing guidelines, and it is very important that these are followed. If insufficient resources are made available for vRealize Operations, it will cease to function correctly!

The latest version of vRealize Operations Manager, version 6.1, supports up to 120,000 objects and 30,000,000 metrics, with 16 nodes in a non-HA configuration. If an HA environment is required then these figures are halved.

VMware publishes links to the most up to date sizing guidelines and spreadsheets at `http://kb.vmware.com/selfservice/microsites/search.do?language=en_US&cmd=displayKC&externalId=2093783`.

vRealize Operations editions and licensing

There are an ever increasing number of ways of consuming and licensing vRealize Operations, and they have evolved quite significantly over time.

Editions

vRealize Operations is available in three **editions**, and these define what functionality and components you are entitled to. The three editions are *Standard*, *Advanced*, and *Enterprise*, and as you move up the range, more features and components are added.

The solution is evolving with every major and minor release, and as functionality is added/removed or moved from one component to another, the capability in each edition can change slightly.

The following table highlights the main capabilities of each edition, with the release of vRealize Operations 6.1. A full and current list of features available in each edition can be found on VMware's website at `http://www.vmware.com/uk/products/vrealize-operations/compare`.

	Standard Edition	Advanced Edition	Enterprise Edition
vRealize Operations Manager	✓	✓	✓
- Custom Dashboards and Reports		✓	✓
- High Availability		✓	✓
- Automated Remediation		✓	✓
- Workload Plans and Rebalancing		✓	✓
- Capacity Model-Driven Analytics		✓	✓
- Host and VM Container Configuration Management	✓	✓	✓
vRealize Operations Management Packs			
- For OS and Infrastructure		✓	✓
- For Applications			✓
Virtual Infrastructure Navigator		✓	✓
End Point Operations/Hyperic		✓	✓
- For OS monitoring		✓	✓
- For Application Monitoring			✓
vRealize Configuration Manager		✓	✓
- For vSphere and VM Containers		✓	✓
- For In-guest Configuration Management			✓

vRealize Operations Standard Edition

This edition is designed for vSphere environments only, and provides the core vRealize Operations Manager platform to deliver the predictive analytics capabilities and associated smart alerts. The alerting framework of symptoms, recommendations, and actions is introduced, as is policy management, so that different SLAs and alerting can be applied to different parts of your environment.

Capacity management of the vSphere environment is also included in the Standard Edition. Within the capacity management framework, capacity projects can be defined to enable you to understand the impact of future workloads changes.

Finally, the first step in configuration management is included, with the ability to assess the compliance of the vSphere hosts and the VM containers against the vSphere Hardening Guidelines.

vRealize Operations Advanced Edition

As well as offering more features as described next, the Advanced Edition provides the additional components, vRealize Configuration Manager, vRealize Hyperic/End Point Operations, and vRealize Infrastructure Navigator.

The key enhancements to vRealize Operations Manager Advanced Edition, over the Standard Edition, is the ability to add infrastructure Management Packs, as well as allowing you to create customized dashboards and reports.

The vRealize Operations Management Pack for Storage Devices is included with the Advanced Edition. This edition also supports third party management packs, including those from Hitachi, EMC, Dell, HP, and Blue Medora (for NetApp).

This ability, to manage performance, health, and capacity of storage in the same place and alongside vSphere Management, is very compelling for the IT administrators I have worked with.

Customized dashboards and reporting mean that you can effectively visualize, report on, and export all the information within vRealize Operations in almost any way and in any context. We will cover this in detail in *Chapter 3*, *Dashboards, Badges, and Widgets* and *Chapter 4*, *Views and Reports*.

The capability to install additional nodes to provide a **High Availability** (**HA**) cluster is enabled with the Advanced Edition.

The capacity projects feature is enhanced with the ability to **commit** capacity projects. This means that all capacity reporting has the committed projects included in the calculation when they report on available capacity and time remaining.

From a configuration management perspective, the vSphere Hardening Guidelines capabilities introduced in the Standard Edition are enhanced, to allow the reporting of the configuration posture with an additional sub-badge, Compliance, under the Risk badge.

vRealize Infrastructure Navigator is added, which provides application discovery and visualization of dependencies between the VMs within your infrastructure. Metadata about applications running on the VMs and the groupings of the VMs as applications within vRealize Infrastructure Navigator, is exposed in vRealize Operations Manager. This can be used to automate dynamic groupings, or as the basis for the construction of alerts and symptoms. We will look at vRealize Infrastructure Navigator in *Chapter 8*, *vRealize Infrastructure Navigator*.

vRealizeHyperic/End Point Operations is also added. This additional solution allows for the collection of the OS metric and property data by vRealize Operations Manager. It also offers the capability to monitor the OS, allowing you through an agent to, for example, monitor specific Windows services and act accordingly if they become unavailable or start to consume too much resource. We will cover the transition of Hyperic to End Point Operations and look at the solution in detail in *Chapter 10*, *End Point Operations*.

Finally, vRealize Configuration Manager for vSphere is included, which allows a rich capability to manage the vSphere hosts and the VM containers configuration, including templates to assess against configuration and regulatory compliance requirements, such as PCI-DSS, HIPAA and SOX.

vRealize Operations Enterprise Edition

The Enterprise Edition extends the management capabilities into the guest OS and into application management.

It extends the licensing in vRealize Configuration Manager to manage the VM guests (OS and Application) and extends vRealizeHyperic/End Point Operations to manage applications such as SQL and Exchange, and bring their metrics and properties into vRealize Operations Manager.

Additional management packs with an application focus are also made available with this edition.

Licensing

There are currently six different ways to license vRealize Operations:

- **Standalone**: Each edition is available in packs of 25 Operating System Instances (OSIs). An OSI is a VM or a physical machine you want to license.

- **vSphere with Operations Management (VSOM)**: VSOM is a license package that includes vSphere Standard, Enterprise, or Enterprise Plus Edition, combined with vSphere Operations Standard Edition. It is available on a per-CPU basis.

- **vRealize Operations Insight**: This is an upgrade to VSOM that upgrades vRealize Operations to the Advanced Edition and adds Log Insight for all the licensed CPUs. Again, this license is provided on a per-CPU basis.

- **vCloud Suite**: There are 3 editions of vCloud Suite - vCloud Suite Standard includes vRealize Operations Standard, vCloud Suite Advanced includes vRealize Operations Advanced, and vCloud Suite Enterprise includes vRealize Operations Enterprise. All are licensed on a per-CPU basis.

- **vRealize Suite**: There are 2 editions of vRealize Suite - vRealize Suite Advanced includes vRealize Operations Advanced, and vRealize Suite Enterprise includes vRealize Operations Enterprise. Both versions of vRealize Suite also include licensing for Log Insight and are available either on a per-CPU basis or in packs of 25 OSIs.
- **vRealize Operations for Horizon**: This is a specific edition designed to support Horizon View VDI environments and is available on a per active VDI session basis.

Mixing licensing

Licenses for vRealize Operations can be mixed in some circumstances.

Per-CPU and per OSI can be mixed, as long as every resource being managed has a valid license associated with it.

vRealize Operations Advanced and Enterprise editions can be mixed on a single vRealize Operations Manager cluster. This is to allow you to use vRealize Operations Advanced to manage your entire estate and have a subset, perhaps your business critical applications, managed with the additional functionality provided by vRealize Operations Enterprise.

The latest information on product licensing is available in the VMware Product Guide at `http://www.vmware.com/files/pdf/vmware-product-guide.pdf`.

Summary

In this chapter, we introduced vRealize Operations Manager and explained how it fits with the rest of the vRealize family. We looked at the operational disciplines of performance, capacity, configuration, and compliance, how vRealize Operations addresses them, and the benefits to the administrator.

We then looked at the architecture scalability and resilience, and finally covered the somewhat complex topics of editions and licensing.

In the next chapter, we will look at how to install and administer vRealize Operations Manager.

2
Install, Configure, and Administer vRealize Operations Manager

This chapter will guide you through installing vRealize Operations, establishing the cluster, and setting the initial configuration, including establishing your initial groups and default policy. Finally, we will look at some of the ongoing administrative tasks needed to keep the solution healthy and running smoothly.

The topics we will cover are:

- Initial planning and preparation
- vApp deployment
- Adding Nodes and High Availability (HA)
- Initial configuration, policies and groups
- Administration of vRealize Operations

 This chapter will only cover the installation of vRealize Operations as a virtual appliance. Installation on Linux and Windows is also possible; however, this needs special consideration, and is outside the scope of this book.

Planning for installation

Before you start installing vRealize Operations, you need to do some planning and preparation. The main areas you need to look at are **product compatibility**, **architecture,** and **sizing**. Due diligence in these areas at this stage will make for a successful implementation of vRealize Operations.

Product compatibility

Ensuring you are installing the solution on compatible equipment, and that the systems you want to manage are compatible, is the first thing to check.

 This chapter refers to the installation of vRealize Operations 6.1. You can find the latest requirements in the release notes for the version you are installing at `https://www.vmware.com/support/pubs/vrealize-operations-manager-pubs.html`.

vRealize Operations is relatively flexible with respect to the interoperability of the older versions of vSphere, so I have rarely come across situations where compatibility with vSphere holds a project up.

The following is a summary of the compatibility requirements:

- **vSphere**: vRealize Operations comes as a **Virtual Appliance (vApp)** and can be installed on an ESX/ESXi host at version 4.0 or later. The host needs to be managed by vCenter Server 4.0 Update 2 or later. vRealize Operations can connect to, and manage, ESX/ESXi 4.0 and vCenter Server 4.0 Update 2 or later.

- **Browser**: You access vRealize Operations using a browser. Most versions of Firefox and Chrome are supported, and I generally recommend using those as they have provided me the best experience. Internet Explorer 10 or 11 is also supported, however, you will experience slower performance.

  From a practical perspective, you need to access vRealize Operations from a device with a good screen resolution and screen size. For lab work, my 15" laptop at 1440 × 900 resolution is about the minimum I would consider. For day to day use, you will benefit from a decent sized external monitor.

  Using a tablet is almost impossible unless you were to build dashboards for specific use cases.

- **VMware products**: The following integrated products are supported:
    - ◦ vCenter Infrastructure Navigator 5.8 and above
    - ◦ vRealize Configuration Manager 5.6 and 5.7.x and 5.8
    - ◦ vRealize Operations Manager for Horizon 6.1.0
    - ◦ vRealize Hyperic 5.8.4.x

Architecture

The building block of vRealize Operations is the **node**. You will build your vRealize Operations cluster out of one or more nodes, depending on your scalability and high availability requirements. Your architecture will also have quite a high dependency on **sizing,** which is covered in the next section.

Sizing

Accurate sizing is very important. Sizing is determined by the number of **objects** you will be managing and the number of **metrics** you will be collecting. If you are just managing a vSphere environment, this is relatively straightforward to calculate; however, if you are going to be adding a number of **Management Packs**, you will need to do more calculations.

The sizing guidelines do change from time to time, and from version to version, so you should always check the following Knowledge Base article for the latest information and sizing spreadsheet: `http://kb.vmware.com/selfservice/ microsites/search.do?language=en_US&cmd=displayKC&externalId=2093783`.

The preceding URL has links to a sizing Knowledge Base article for each version of vRealize Operations. Each of these articles has a sizing spreadsheet that can be downloaded.

The sizing spreadsheet is fairly straightforward and contains three worksheets.

Overall Scaling Table

This worksheet highlights how many objects and metrics each size of node can support. You need to ensure the nodes in your design are large enough to support the quantity of objects and metrics in your environment, and do not breach the maximums in the Overall Scaling Table.

Sizing Guide – basic

This is suitable for simple deployments against environments in which you are only going to do vSphere monitoring.

Sizing Guide – advanced

This should be used if you are using any additional Management Packs. Unfortunately, there is not much detail in the sizing spreadsheet on the quantity of metrics each Management Pack collects. This means that you will need to check the Management Pack documentation to find out how many metrics are collected for each object type that the Management Pack monitors, and multiply that by the number of each object type.

Scaling up and scaling out

The following screenshot shows a typical sizing example. You can see that with **High Availability** disabled, you would have a choice of deploying with two small nodes, one medium node, or one large node.

System Sizing Estimate

Input

	High Availability		DISABLED	
	Data Retention (Months)		6	

vRealize Operations Manager Objects		# Resources	# Metrics / Resource	Collected metrics
vCenter Objects				
	Virtual centers	1	88	88
	Datacenters	1	75	75
	Clusters	16	107	1,712
	Virtual machines	2,000	250	500,000
	Hosts	100	450	45,000
	Datastores	50	73	3,650
	Total vCenter Objects	2,168	vCenter Metrics:	550,525
EMC VNX Arrays				
	Total EMC Arrays objects	250	EMC VNX Metrics:	10,000

Recommendation Summary (options are provided for different node configurations)

Node form factor	Number of nodes	Data disk size per node(GB)	IOPs per node	Total vCPUs	Total memory(GB)
Extra Small	Not supported	Not supported	Not supported	Not supported	Not supported
Small	2	204	432	8	32
Medium	1	393	865	8	32
Large	1	418	865	16	48

Generally speaking, I prefer to scale up before scaling out as it decreases the complexity of the solution, and means that you have fewer moving parts.

An exception to this rule would be if you needed a larger number of concurrent user sessions. These are limited to 4 per node, so if in the preceding example, I needed 8 concurrent user sessions, I would choose to deploy 2 small nodes instead of 1 medium node or 1 large node.

> The limit on the number of concurrent users per node has relaxed slightly with the release of vRealize Operations 6.1. Further guidance is expected, particularly for large multi-node clusters. Guidance for each version of vRealize Operations is documented and updated at the sizing URL referenced earlier.

High Availability

The final consideration is **High Availability (HA)**, which was initially discussed in *Chapter 1*, *Introduction to vRealize Operations Manager*.

The first node installed in a cluster is the **Master node**. When you implement an HA cluster, one of the nodes will become a **Master Replica node** to take over the Master role should the Master node fail.

When it comes to deployment, you should ensure that the Master and the Master Replica nodes are hosted on separate hardware to ensure continued operations in the event of a host failure.

> Due to the in-memory Gemfire based database, vRealize Operations nodes need to be closely coupled and generally located in the same data center. Check the sizing URL referenced earlier for network latency requirements between the nodes and the remote collectors.

So, once you have put your numbers into the sizing spreadsheet, worked out how many nodes you are going to need, and what size nodes you are going to install, it is time to install vRealize Operations.

Installing vRealize Operations Manager

As vRealize Operations is provided as a virtual appliance, installation is relatively straightforward. Installation involves the following main activities:

- Install the required nodes
- Configure the Master node
- Add the Data nodes
- Enable the Master Replica node (optional)
- Configure the installation

Deploy the vRealize Operations nodes

First you need to download the vRealize Operations Manager virtual appliance code .ova file from My VMware, and store it somewhere from where you can access it with the vSphere Web Client.

 If you do not have a license for vRealize Operations, you can register for an evaluation and get the code from `http://www.vmware.com/go/try-vrealize-ops-dl-en`.

You will use the **vSphere Web Client** to install the nodes, and will need to have sufficient permissions to deploy the OVF templates. The permissions required in vCenter Server are:

- **All Privileges | Datastore | Allocate space**
- **All Privileges | Network | Assign network**
- **All Privileges | Virtual machine | Configuration | Add new disk**
- **All Privileges | Virtual machine | Configuration | Advanced**
- **All Privileges | vApp | Import**

You can find full information on how to create a role with the above permissions in the following VMware Knowledge Base article: `http://kb.vmware.com/selfservice/microsites/search.do?language=en_US&cmd=displayKC&externalId=2105932`

Each node will require a static **IP address.** I would recommend that you also create **DNS** entries so that you can use **FQDNs** across your management infrastructure.

Log into the vSphere Web Client, right-click on the cluster where you want to install your nodes, and select **Deploy OVF Template** to start the deployment wizard:

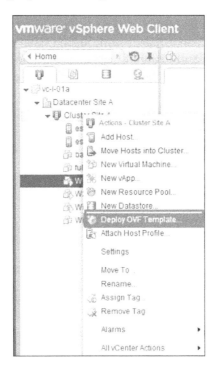

Now complete the steps in the wizard, as follows:

1. Click on **Browse** and browse to the location where you stored the virtual appliance `.ova` file. Click on the file and **Open** it. Click on **Next**.

2. Tick the **Accept extra configuration options** tick box, review the virtual appliance details, and click on **Next**.

3. Click on **Accept** to accept the EULA and then click on **Next**.

4. Next you need to choose the data center or the folder in which you want to install the node. You can also change the name of your Virtual Appliance in this panel. Browse your folder structure, select the appropriate folder or the data center, change the name of your Virtual Applicance if required, and click on **Next**.

5. Now use the drop down to choose **configuration size** of the node that you decided in Sizing earlier, and click on **Next**.

6. Now you need to choose the storage that the node will be deployed on, and whether you want to install using **Thin Provisioned**, **Thick Provisioned Lazy Zeroed**, or **Thick Provision Eager Zeroed** disk format. The recommendation from VMware is to deploy Thick Provision Eager Zeroed, if possible, for best performance, although, I have regularly used Thin Provisioned in labs and Proof of Concepts with no noticeable performance issues. You can also optionally select a **VM Storage Policy**. Once all the options are selected, click on **Next**.

7. The next step is to setup the **Destination** network you want to connect your node to. Click on the drop down arrow to select the appropriate network. Once selected, click on **Next** to continue the wizard.

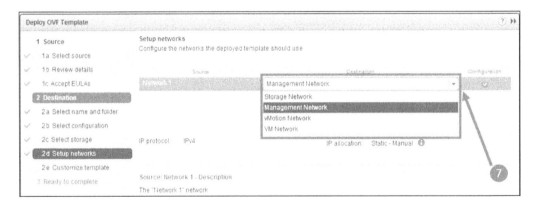

8. Now we need to configure the network settings. Click on the arrow next to **Networking Properties** to expand the networking properties section. You will need to add the following IP properties:

   ○ Default Gateway
   ○ DNS Server(s)
   ○ IP address of the node (Network 1 IP address)
   ○ Netmask

The recommendation is to use static IP addressing, however, if you leave these fields blank, DHCP can be used. There is a checkbox for selecting IPV6 for DHCP if you wish to use this.

9. If needed, change the timezone. The preferred approach from VMware is to use the default of UTC. If you do change this, you need to ensure that you have consistent settings across all your nodes in the cluster. Click on **Next** to continue.

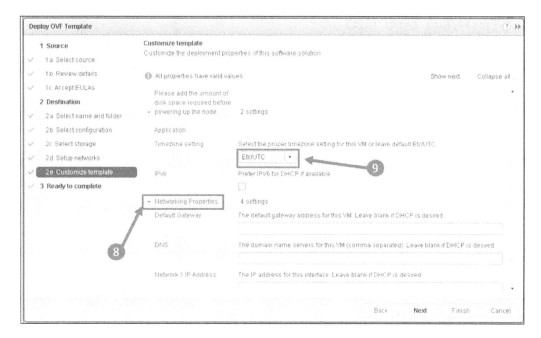

10. In the **Ready to complete** panel, you can review your settings and optionally select the checkbox to power on after deployment. Click on **Finish** to complete the wizard and deploy the node.

    You can watch the node deployment complete in the tasks window of the vSphere Web Client.

11. Once the node is deployed, depending on the disk space requirements from the sizing spreadsheet, you may need to add further diskspace to the node. You do this in the vSphere Web client by navigating to the Virtual Appliance and changing its hardware settings, either by:

    ° Increasing the size of Hard Disk 2, or

    ° Adding another disk

12. The node can now be powered on.

Once the node is deployed and powered on, it will take a few minutes for it to fully boot up. This initial boot will be complete when the console displays the message **Welcome to the vRealize Operations Manager Appliance**.

While you are waiting for this message to appear, you can follow the preceding steps as many times as you need to, until you have installed the number of nodes required for your cluster.

Establish the cluster

Now that all your nodes are installed, you can create the vRealize Operations cluster. The first step is to create the **Master node** using the Setup Wizard.

Creating the Master node

First, using your browser, navigate to the IP address or FQDN of the node that you want to become the Master node. That will bring up the **Get Started** screen. Click on **New Installation** to start the installation of a new cluster.

You can optionally use the Express Configuration option; however, if you do so you won't have the option to customize the certificates, rename your node, or configure NTP. This is possibly fine for a lab environment, but I do prefer to at least configure NTP properly, as it is something you will need if you ever want to add High Availability or additional data nodes.

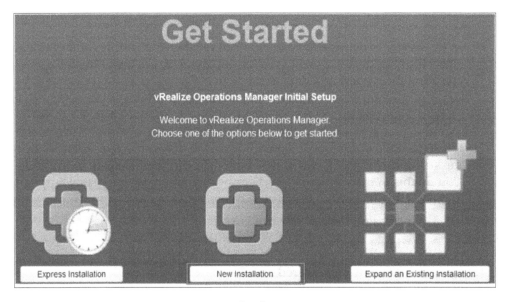

The **Initial Setup Wizard** will appear and you will need to complete the following steps:

1. Click on **Next** to get started.

2. Choose a new password for the internal **admin** account, taking into consideration the password strength requirements on the input panel. Click on **Next** to continue.

 Please do remember this password and keep it in a safe place! Even after your cluster is fully established and has been running for some time, you will need **admin** access to perform some administrative functions.

3. Install your **certificate**. To use the default certificate, click on **Next** to continue. To use your own certificate:
   - Click on **Install a certificate**
   - Click on **Browse** to locate your certificate `.PEM` file
   - Enter the certificate **password** and the **alias** name
   - Click on **Upload**
   - Review the information about your certificate and click on **Next** to continue

 If you want to use your own certificate, there are a number of requirements that are listed on the panel. There are more detailed requirements and examples available in the *vRealize Operations Manager vApp Deployment Guide*.

4. In the **Deployment Settings** panel, enter a name for the node. For example, **vROps-Master**.

5. In the **NTP Server Address** box, enter the IP address or FQDN of your **NTP server** and click on **Add**. If you have multiple NTP sources, repeat this step for each one. Click on **Next** to continue.

6. Click on **Finish** in the final panel and your cluster will start its initial configuration process.

Add Data nodes

If your cluster requires more than one node, you now need to add the additional **Data nodes**.

First, using your browser, navigate to the IP address or FQDN of the node that you want to become a new Data node. That will bring up the **Get Started** screen. Click on **Expand an Existing Installation** to add the Data node.

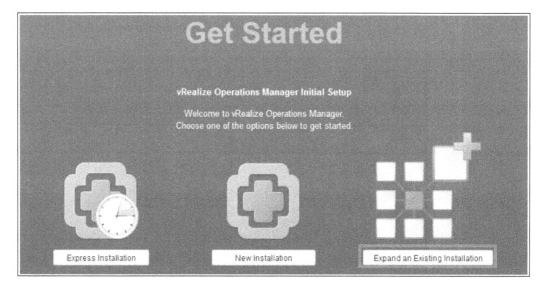

The Initial Setup Wizard will appear and you will need to complete the following steps:

1. Click on **Next** to get started.

2. In the **Node Settings and Cluster Information** panel, enter a name for the node. For example, **vROps-Data-1**. Leave **Node Type** in the drop down box as **Data**.

3. Enter the IP address or FQDN of the cluster Master node and click on **Validate**. This will load the certificate from the Master node.

4. Tick the **Accept this certificate** box and click on **Next** to continue.

5. Enter the **password** you created earlier for the **admin** account and click on **Next**.

 You will see another option to use a **passphrase** instead. This can be used if the cluster is already fully established and you need to add a node for capacity. The passphrase is created by the admin user in the Admin UI of the Master node.

6. Click on **Finish** to complete the wizard. The Data node will be added to the cluster.

Repeat the preceding steps until all your Data nodes have been added.

Configure High Availability

The final step in establishing the cluster is to optionally configure **High Availability (HA)**. To do this, you have to change one of the Data node's role to Master Replica.

The Master Replica will be, as its name implies, a complete replica, or copy, of the Master node. Should the Master node fail, the Master Replica will take over automatically.

To enable HA, carry out the following steps:

1. If you do not have the page still open following the installation of the Master node, browse to the **Admin UI** of the Master node using `https://IP-address-or-FQDN-of-Master-Node/admin`.

2. Log in using **admin** and the **password** you set during the installation.

3. Click on **Enable**.

4. In the **Enable High Availability** panel, select the node you want to be the Replica Master, tick the **Enable High Availability for this cluster** check box, and click on **OK** to complete.

Starting the cluster

Once you have deployed all your nodes, installed the Master node, added the Data nodes, and turned on HA if required, the final task is to start your cluster and run the final steps of initial configuration.

In the Admin UI of the Master node, click on **Start vRealize Operations Manager**. A dialogue box will advise you to confirm that you have enough nodes to manage your environment, but as you have followed a rigorous sizing process, you can just click **Yes** to continue, and start the cluster.

The initial start-up process may take as long as 30 minutes, so be patient and don't make any more changes until the cluster status is **Online,** as shown in the following image:

Finalizing initial configuration

Now that the cluster is **Online,** you can log into the main **vRealize Operations UI.** Browse to `http://IP-address-or-FQDN-of-Master-Node` and enter the login credentials of **admin** and the **password** you set during the installation.

In the previous versions of vCenter Operations, there were three UIs – the Admin UI, the vSphere UI, and the Custom UI.

From vRealize Operations 6.0 onward, we still have the Admin UI, which is the UI we have been using so far; however, the vSphere and Custom UIs have been combined into a new single UI, the vRealize Operations UI.

We will spend most of the rest of this book in the vRealize Operations UI.

A final configuration wizard will open and the following steps should be completed:

1. Click on **Next** to start the wizard.

In vRealize Operations 6.0.x, there was an option to migrate from vCenter Operations 5.8 at this stage. With the introduction of vRealize Operations 6.1, this option is no longer available in this wizard. We will cover migrations later in this chapter.

2. Tick the check box to accept the EULA and click on **Next**.

3. If you have a vRealize Operations license key then select **Product Key**, enter the license key, and click on **Validate**. Alternatively, select **Product Evaluation,** which will license the solution for 60 days for you to evaluate it. Click on **Next** to continue.

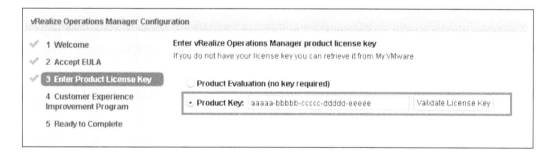

4. Optionally, select the **Customer Experience Improvement Program** check box and click on **Next** to continue.

5. Click on **Finish** to complete.

This completes the installation of vRealize Operations. The next step is to install and configure **Solutions** to connect to the resources and start managing them.

Configure the vSphere solution

The next step in installing vRealize Operations is to connect it to your vCenter(s), and the way to do this is to configure the **VMware vSphere Solution**.

Solutions are how vRealize connects to resources to manage them. A solution is usually delivered by way of a separately installed **Management Pack**. The VMware vSphere Solution is, however, installed automatically during the initial installation of vRealize Operations Manager, so there is no further code installation required, just configuration.

> The **End Point Operations** solution is also installed automatically during vRealize Operations installation. We will cover other solutions in *Chapter 7, vRealize Operations Manager Solutions* and the End Point Operations solution in detail in *Chapter 10, End Point Operations*.

Solutions, or Management Packs, usually contain the following:

- **Adapter(s)**: A plug in to vRealize Operations that connects to the resource being managed, and collects metrics and properties.

- **Dashboards**: Pre-configured dashboards in vRealize Operations to help troubleshoot and visualize the resource being managed.

- **Content**: **Alerts**, **Symptoms**, **Views**, **Actions**, and **Reports** specific to the resource being managed.

In the vRealize Operations UI, click on the **Administration** icon highlighted in the following screenshot:

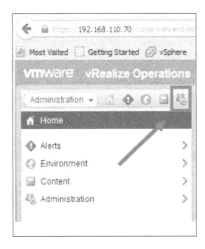

Solutions is the first item on the **Administration** panel, so it will already be selected. You will see the **End Point Operations** (labelled Operating Systems/Remote Monitoring) and the VMware vSphere Solutions, in the **Solutions** panel on the right.

> A note on the **credentials** required by vRealize Operations:
>
> vRealize Operations requires **credentials** to connect to your vCenter(s). There are two type of credentials that can be configured:
>
> - **Standard Credentials**: These are used by the adapter to log into your vCenter(s), and collect metrics and properties. The login ID used by the adapter needs to have at least read permissions to the objects it is collecting.
> - **Registration Credentials**: These are optional, but recommended if the standard credentials do not have vCenter administrative permissions.
>
> Allowing vRealize Operations to register with vCenter will enable it to apply the vRealize Operations plug-in to the vSphere Web Client. This means that you will be able to see things such as the Health status of your VMs, and launch vRealize Operations from the vSphere Web Client.

Click on the **VMware vSphere** solution to select it and then the cog icon to start the solution configuration.

The VMware vSphere solution consists of two adapters:

- **vCenter Adapter**: For collection of the metrics and properties of everything managed by a vCenter
- **vCenter Python Actions Adapter**: Used by **Actions** within vRealize Operations to perform actions on vSphere objects. For example, to reconfigure, or power on a VM.

Configuring the vCenter adapter

The configuration panel for the vCenter adapter is shown first. Click on the arrow next to advanced Settings so that you can see all the 12 fields of this panel. They should be filled in as follows:

1. **Display name**: What the adapter will be called. For example, `Production vCenter 1`.

2. **Description**: A free form text field you can use to add a description.

3. **vCenter Server**: The IP address or FQDN of the first vCenter you want to connect the adapter to

4. **Credential**: Click on the green plus icon to add a credential.

The manage credential panel will require the following information:

  - **Credential Name**: A free from field for you to name the credential. For example, `Production vCenter 1 Admin User`.

  - **User Name**: A user with sufficient permissions to collect the data.

  - **Password**: The password for the data collection user.

Click on OK to save the credential and continue.

At this point, you should test your connection to vCenter by clicking on the **Test Connection** button. A dialogue box showing you the details of your vCenter's certificate will appear. Click on **OK** to continue if you trust the certificate. If you have configured the credentials correctly, you will get a dialogue box saying **Test was successful**. Click on **OK** to continue. Now let's look at the **Advanced Settings** options:

5. **Collector/Groups**: Use this drop down option to select the specific node or Collector Group you want the adapter to run on. The Default Collector Group contains all the nodes in the cluster and is generally the option you should select.

You may select a specific node where you have particular sizing or design considerations, such as knowing the adapter is going to collect significantly more metrics in the future, and you wish to avoid an adapter rebalance.

Collector Groups are used to group Remote Collectors together for high availability purposes, and are discussed in the *Administration Panel* section towards the end of this chapter.

6. **Auto Discovery**: If this is set to `True`, then any new objects added to vSphere after this initial configuration will be automatically added to vRealize Operations. If it is set to `False`, they won't. This is generally used post-installation if, for example, you want to pause discovery or if you are doing some maintenance work, and don't want the new items to appear in vRealize Operations.

7. **Process Change Events**: vRealize Operations collects change events such as **VMotion Initiated** or **VM reconfigured** from vCenter. You can turn this collection off by setting this field to `False` from the default setting of `True`. Again, this is probably most useful if you are doing some maintenance and don't want to clog vRealize Operations with un-needed event information.

8. **Enable Collecting vSphere Distributed Switch**, **Virtual Machine Folder,** and **vSPhere Distributed Port Group**: If any of these are set to `False`, it disables the collection of that object type. This allows you to reduce your dataset size by disabling the collection of object types you may be less interested in.

9. **Exclude Virtual Machines from Capacity Calculations**: This will reduce the nightly analytics load and would generally be used in implementations that were reaching the limits of scalability.

10. **Maximum Number of Virtual Machines Collected**: This limits the number of Virtual Machines the adapter can collect for. This would be used if you were worried about scalability and wanted to govern the adapter's collection capability.

11. **Registration User**: If you are using a registration user, as described in the previous tip box, you enter its login details here.

12. **Registration Password**: This is the password for the registration user.

Once you have completed the panel, click on **Save Settings**. Before we click on **Next** in the wizard, we should configure the Python Adapter.

Configuring the vCenter Python Adapter

The vCenter Python Adapter provides the **Actions** functionality to provide remediation capabilities. We will cover Actions in *Chapter 5, Alerts, Symptoms, Recommendations, and Actions*.

Click on **vCenter Python Actions Adapter** at the top of the **Manage Solution** panel.

The vCenter Python Adapter has only 5 fields to fill in. They are a subset of the vCenter Adapter fields, so follow the steps in the previous section, changing **Display name** and **Description** to something appropriate for the Python Adapter. The **credential** will require vCenter administrative permissions.

Once complete, click on **Save Settings** and then click on **Next** to bring up a final panel that will define your initial monitoring goals.

Defining monitoring goals

The final step in configuring the vCenter Solution is to define your **initial monitoring goals**. This will create your **Default policy**. There are five sections in the **Define monitoring goals** panel to consider:

- **Which objects do you want to be alerted on?**: The default is all vSphere objects, but if you want to just be alerted on infrastructure, or just on VMs, click on the radio button to change the selection.

- **Which type of alerts do you want to enable?**: The default is **Health**, **Risk,** and **Efficiency**. If you want to remove any of these alerts, untick the check-box.

- **Overcommit CPU in your Environment?**: This will define how **capacity planning** for CPU is set up. The default of **Yes** to overcommit CPU is generally the most appropriate and will set CPU to a Demand capacity model.

- **Configure Memory Capacity Based on?**: This will define how capacity planning for memory is set up. The three options are:
  - ○ **True Demand – Most aggressive**: This will set memory to a **Demand** based capacity model.
  - ○ **Memory Consumed – vSphere Default**: This will set the capacity model to be based on memory consumed by vSphere as reported in vCenter.
  - ○ **Do not Overcommit – Most Conservative**: This is a pure **Allocation** model.

> We will cover **Demand** and **Allocation** capacity models and how you tune your policies in depth in *Chapter 6, Capacity Planning and Capacity Projects*.
>
> As described in that chapter, although the default of **Memory Consumed** is fine, there may be occasions where you would want to start with a pure **Allocation** model without overcommit.

- **Enable vSphere Hardening Alerts**: This will enable the out of the box vSphere Hardening Guidelines alerts. The default of **No** will be fine for now. We will enable them during an exercise later in this chapter.

Once you have made your selections, click on **Next** and then **Finish** to complete the configuration. You have now completed configuring the VMware vSphere Solution and you will now see it collecting and receiving data in the **Solution Details** panel, as seen in the following screenshot:

Migrating from vCenter Operations 5.8.x

vRealize Operations offers the capability to migrate from vCenter Operations 5.8.x; however, you can only migrate from vCenter Operations 5.8.x to vRealize Operations 6.0.x.

If you want to migrate from vCenter Operations 5.8.x to vRealize Operation 6.1, you must first migrate to vRealize Operations 6.0.3 and then perform an upgrade to vRealize Operations 6.1.

Migrations are potentially complex operations – the *vRealize Operations Manager vApp Deployment and Configuration Guide* for vRealize Operations 6.0.3 has information on how to migrate and, more importantly, details on whether you ought to engage VMware's Professional Services Organization (PSO) for design and migration advice.

If you already have vCenter Operations 5.8.x, you should consider the migration option if:

- You want to retain the metrics data that you have already collected from your estate
- Your current operational practices make extensive use of the health, alerting, and capacity planning features
- Metrics or data from vCenter Operations is passed to other systems
- Extensive custom content, such as, policies, custom dashboards, and groupings have been created and you wish to maintain these

Not all data and features will be migrated – check the *vRealize Operations Manager vApp Deployment and Configuration Guide* for a full list of data and features that will, or will not, be migrated, or that may be changed. The guide also includes a full and detailed list of the pre-requisites you need in place.

The migration itself is a **side-by-side** operation, and you can keep your existing vCenter Operations system operating until you have completed the operation and are satisfied that vRealize Operations is operating how you need it to.

Adapters themselves will not be migrated, so before you start the migration, you will need to install the appropriate solutions on your vRealize Operations cluster.

Taking everything into consideration, I would recommend to generally avoid migration unless you have significant intellectual property, or operational practices, baked into your vCenter Operations 5.8 installation, or if you absolutely must keep your historical metrics.

Configuring groups and policies

Groups and **policies** are key to configuring vRealize Operations to meet your **operational imperatives** and **service level agreements (SLAs)**.

If you take the simple example of an organization with **production** and **test** environments, it is usually the case that you will operate them in different ways.

For example, in a test environment, you may not be interested in receiving non-critical alerts, and you may overcommit significantly your CPU and memory resources. In a production environment, you will more likely be interested in receiving more alerts, and you may adopt a more conservative allocation policy for CPU or for memory resources.

We use policies to define how features in vRealize Operations Solutions operate, with respect to capabilities such as **alerts** and **capacity planning**. We use Groups to assign policies to groups of objects. So in the preceding example, we may create a grouping of all the objects in our test environment and attach a *Test Environment* policy to it.

Policies

There are three main areas to consider with respect to policies:

- **Solutions**: When you add a solution to vRealize Operations, it will typically add the policy configuration options for that solution.
- **Object type**: Every object in vRealize Operations is classified as an object type. For example, vSphere clusters are classified as **Cluster Compute Resource**. Every solution will add one or more object types, to represent the resources it is monitoring.
- **Policy elements**: Every object type type can be individually represented in your policies, and contains a number of policy elements. These determine the individual feature being controlled and its value.

For example, the object type, **Cluster Compute Resource** includes policy elements to define items such as:

- The conditions under which badges change color
- Which alerts are associated with the object
- How capacity should be calculated
- Which metrics should be collected

Base Settings policy

The **Base Settings policy** is a great place to start looking at policies. This policy is the initial definition of policy coming from all the solutions installed. It's important to note that you cannot change the Base Settings policy; it is just the starting point.

To view the Base Settings policy:

1. Click on the **Administration** icon.
2. Click on **Policies** in the **Administration** pane.
3. Click on the **Policy Library** tab.
4. To see all the additional policies, expand the list of policies by clicking on the *plus* icon next to **Base Settings**.
5. Click on **Base Settings** to select the policy.
6. You can browse through the policy settings in the policy pane at the bottom.

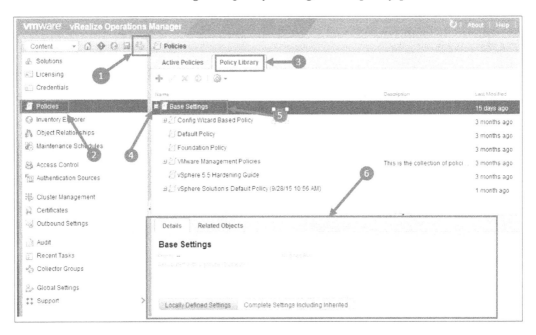

Other policies

Every policy, except the **Base Settings** policy, is a definition of policy changes relative to the base policy. A policy can be thought of as settings that override the base settings.

For example, the policy for Cluster Compute Resource sets the value at which the Workload badge turns red, at 95. If you would rather the badge turns red at, say, a value of 98, you would change that setting in one of your policies.

Default policy

The **default policy** is the initial policy that is applied to every object in vRealize Operations. Out of the box, the default policy is *blank* – that is to say, there are no changes to the **Base Policy** settings, so every object will inherit the base policy setting.

When you configured the vSphere solution earlier in this chapter and defined your initial monitoring goals, it created and applied a new default policy, called *vSphere Solution's Default Policy (date/time of installation)*. It also added changes to reflect your goals. For example, if you took the option to **Overcommit CPU**, this policy will have set the CPU capacity controls to **Demand** for relevant resource types in the policy.

Creating a new policy

Policies that you create can be based on the Base Settings policy, or you can use an existing policy as their starting point. If you use an existing policy, then your new policy will inherit all the characteristics of that existing policy.

This policy **nesting** allows you to have, say, a **default policy** for all the objects in your environment, with **additional** policies for the other groups of objects, with minor variance from the default policy.

In the following example, we are going to turn on alerts for vSphere Hardening Guidelines, to provide additional monitoring for servers in our DMZ.

To start, click on **vSphere Solution's Default Policy (date/time of installation)** to select it and then click on the **Add New Policy** *plus* sign to add a policy:

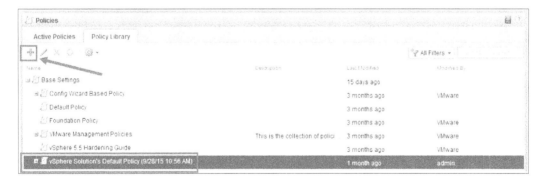

Each policy has 8 sections to complete (to navigate from one to another, simply click on the section heading):

1. **Getting Started**: Add an appropriate entry into the **Name** field, for example, **vSphere Hardening**, and optionally, provide a **description**. Note the **Start with** drop down. As we have started with **vSphere Solution's Default Policy**, this is already selected.

2. **Select Base Policies:** You don't often have to build your new policy from scratch. When you install **Solutions** into vRealize Operations, additional policy templates will often be installed with them for you to use.

    If you want to select one of these as the starting point for your new policy, you simply select one from the drop down list and click on **Apply**.

    For this policy, however, we will start with a blank policy, so click on the next section.

3. **Analysis Settings**: For each object type, you can override how vRealize Operations analyses **Health**, **Risk**, and **Efficiency**. We will cover these in future chapters, so let's go to the next section for now.

4. **Workload Automation**: This is a new feature introduced in vRealize Operations 6.1. There are **Workload Automation** alerts that look for unbalanced resources in the container objects. In this section of the policy, you define your approach to workload automation:

    ○   **Balance Workloads**: How aggressively you want the workloads to be balanced across the container?

    ○   **Consolidate Workloads**: Whether you want **Workload Automation** to recommend that you collapse your workloads to fewer hosts for efficiency reasons

5. **Collect Metrics and Properties**: **Metrics** and **Properties** are collected for every object type. In this section, you can select which metrics and properties are collected. For example, you may want to collect fewer metrics in a development environment. We don't need to make any changes to this section for this new policy.

6. **Alert / Symptom Definitions**: In this section, we define which alerts and attributes are used in the policy. The **vSphere Hardening** alerts are, by default, not used unless you set them when you define your monitoring goals. So if you did not set them there, we can add them now:

    1. There are a large number of alerts listed, so type `Hardening` into the filter box and hit return to just see the hardening alerts

    2. You will see that they both have a state of *disabled*, based on inheritance

3. Select the **State** drop down, and for each of them, change the value to **Local** enabled, designated by the green tick

7. **Custom Profiles**: In the **Capacity Planning** dashboards, object types can have profiles that describe **average**, **large**, **medium**, and **small** examples of those objects. These are used to give you an indication of how many of these can be deployed in a parent container.

   For example, the Capacity Planning dashboard for a Cluster Compute Resource may show how many average, large, medium, and small Virtual Machines can be installed in the remaining available capacity.

   Custom profiles can be created to define custom object sizes, in addition to the calculated average, large, medium, and small sizes. For example, you may define a custom profile to represent your Microsoft Exchange servers so you can see how many of these can still be installed on a given cluster.

   This Policy section allows you to enable and disable these custom profiles for objects the policy is applied to.

8. **Apply Policy to Groups:** You can apply policies to groups of objects by selecting the groups here. We will do this later when we create the group for this new policy.

9. Click on **Save** to complete your first policy. You will see that your new policy is a child of the default policy. You can see the details of your policy by browsing the lower policy panel.

In the subsequent chapters of this book, we will cover the policy options relevant to those chapters. For example, in *Chapter 6, Capacity Planning and Capacity Projects*, we will look in detail at how the policies can be crafted to meet our capacity planning objectives.

Custom groups

In the previous section, we examined how policies affect how vRealize Operations acts. For example, in the Alert/Symptom Definition section of a policy, we showed how you could enable or disable specific alerts, such as the vSphere Hardening Guidelines.

When you create a new policy, it is because you only want to apply that policy to a subset of your estate. If you want to apply it to your entire estate, you just change the default policy.

You create Custom Groups, representing a subset of your estate, to apply these additional policies to.

This isn't the only reason for using Custom Groups. You group objects together for the following main reasons:

- As described earlier, Custom Groups are the constructs that the different policies outside of the default policy are applied to. So, if you have a policy for the *Test* systems, then you would generally group these in a *Test Systems* functional group.

- **Service views** can be created using groupings. For example, an application may be made up of Web, Application, and Database servers, which you may want to group together so you can get a view of the **Health**, **Risk**, and **Efficiency** of the service as a whole.

Groups can also be created by vRealize Infrastructure Navigator. We will look at vRealize Infrastructure Navigator in *Chapter 8, vRealize Infrastructure Navigator*.

Creating a Custom Group and applying a policy

In this section, we will show how you can create a group of VMs and Hosts, and apply the policy you just created to that grouping. To start, click on the **Environment** icon and then on the plus icon to add a group:

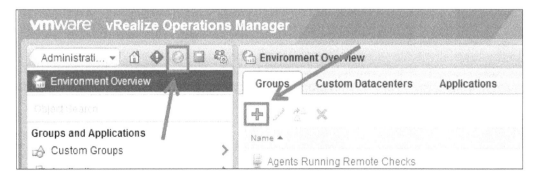

The **New group** panel will appear as follows:

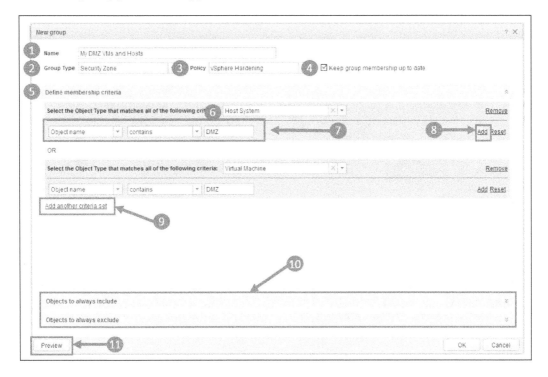

You define your new group as follows:

1. **Name**: Give the group an appropriate name.

2. **Group Type**: This is a field used to categorize or identify the group. In this case, I have used the built in **Security Zone** group type.

3. **Policy**: Here you select the policy you want to apply to the group. I have selected the **vSphere Hardening** policy I just created.

4. **Keep group membership up to date**: If you tick this box, then when new objects that meet the membership criteria are created, they will automatically be added to the group.

5. **Define membership criteria**: This section contains a very rich set of options for defining the membership of your group. You build membership up as follows:

6. Select the Object Type, in this case, **Host Systems**.

7. Select the **Criteria**: There is a very rich set of criteria you can choose from, including **object relationships**, **properties**, and **metrics**. Take some time to browse through the various options. For this first group, I have kept it simple and am looking for **Host System** objects with *DMZ* in their name.

8. If you select **Add**, this will add a second criteria, and both criteria will have to be true. This can be considered a Boolean **AND** operation.

9. In my example, I have selected **Add another criteria set**, which consists of **Virtual Machine** objects with *DMZ* in their name. This can be considered a Boolean **OR** operation.

   To summarize, my membership criteria is **Hosts** or **Virtual Machines** with *DMZ* in their name.

10. You can also include or exclude specific objects. For example, I may have an object in my DMZ that does not have *DMZ* in its name. I will need to manually add it or use another **OR** criteria set.

11. Finally, you can click on the **Preview** button to preview the group membership, in order to check that your criteria is correct.

To complete the group creation, click on **OK**. You have created your first custom group and applied a policy to it. You will find yourself using groups and policies a lot within vRealize Operations, and I will refer to them quite a lot in the future chapters.

Managing vRealize Operations

Administration of vRealize Operations is done in two places, the **Administration panel** of the vRealize Operations UI or the **Admin UI**.

Administration panel

We used the administration panel earlier, when we were installing the vSphere solution and creating our first policy. The panel is also used for:

- **Licensing**: Installing vRealize Operations licenses and applying them to the objects.

- **Credentials**: A central point for managing the credentials you create for your solutions.

- **Inventory Explorer**: A list of all the objects in the environment. You can manually delete and edit the groups of objects here.

- **Object Relationships**: There are hierarchical relations between the objects, and these are generally created by the **Solutions** you install. You can view and change those **relationships** here.

- **Maintenance Schedules**: You can put objects into ad hoc or scheduled **maintenance mode**. When in maintenance mode, their metrics are not collected and they are not alerted on. This is where you define the scheduled maintenance windows.

- **Access Control** and **Authentication Sources**: Here you define which users have access, and can perform which actions against the objects in vRealize Operations. Access can be granted to Local Users, vCenter Users through SSO, or LDAP users, for example, to Active Directory users.

- **Cluster Management**: Here you can monitor and manage the vRealize Operations cluster.

- **Certificates**: vRealize Operations certificates are managed here.

- **Outbound Alert settings**: Alerts can be sent outbound using **SNMP**, **Email** or to **Log Files** or a **REST API**. This is configured here.

- **Audit** and **Recent Tasks**: A log of all activities can be viewed here, as well as reports on **User Permissions**, **System status,** and **Recent Tasks**.

- **Collector Groups**: If you are using **Remote Collectors**, you can group the Collectors together here. If a Collector fails, the Adapter on that Collector will automatically move to another Collector in the group. The vRealize Operations Cluster creates a default Collector group for all the adapters in the main cluster.

- **Global Settings**: Various parameters such as user timeout, data retention, and object history can be set here, as well as whether **Dynamic Thresholds** (**DT**) and capacity calculations are turned on.

- **Support**: In the support section, you can review all the vRealize Operations logs and generate **Support Bundles** if you need to send the logs to VMware support. The DT and **Redescribe** processes can also be initiated here.

Admin UI

The Admin UI is accessed through `https://IP-address-or-FQDN-of-Node/admin`, and is available on every node. In the Admin UI, you can do the following:

- **System Status**: Monitor the status of your nodes and cluster, and take the nodes and cluster offline. Here you can also enable HA, if you have not done so already.

- **Software Update**: Update the vRealize Operations code. Upgrades are delivered as a .PAK file and are generally a very straightforward operation, although care must be taken that all your Solutions installed are fully compatible with any upgrade before applying it.

- **Support**: All the vRealize Operations log files can be viewed here, and support bundles can be created if the logs need to be sent to VMware support.

Summary

In this chapter, we looked at how we can plan for and deploy vRealize Operations Manager. We showed how we can connect vRealize Operations Manager to our vSphere environment to start monitoring it.

We also described what policies are and how they work, created our first policy, and showed how it can be attached to a Custom Group.

Finally, we highlighted the various administrative tasks that we will use to manage our vRealize Operations Manager environment.

In the next chapter, we will start to look at how we can use vRealize Operations to manage our infrastructure.

3
Dashboards, Badges, and Widgets

In this chapter, we will start using vRealize Operations to manage our environment. We will start with an orientation of the UI to get familiar with the structure, the dashboards, and how to navigate the environment.

While we discover the dashboards, we will learn about how badges work in vRealize Operations, what drives their behavior, and how they should be used and interpreted.

Finally, we will introduce custom dashboards and describe how they can be built up using the widgets and views that are available.

The major topics that will be covered include:

- UI and navigation overview
- Major badges
- Alerts and Recommendations pane
- Out of the Box (OOTB) dashboards
- Custom dashboards and widget interactions

The vRealize Operations UI

As discussed in the previous chapter, there are two UIs: the vRealize Operations UI and the Admin UI. You can navigate to the vRealize Operations UI by browsing to the IP address or FQDN of any of your cluster nodes. The vRealize Operations UI replaces the vSphere UI and Custom UI we had with vCenter Operations 5.x.

Advanced capabilities in the vRealize Operations UI are now unlocked using a license key for the Advanced or Enterprise editions of vRealize Operations, as opposed to having to navigate to an alternate UI.

Orientation and navigation

When you login to vRealize Operations, the console will display two main panes.

The left pane is used to navigate around vRealize Operations and the right pane shows information or dashboards relevant to where you have navigated to. There are five main areas you can navigate to by selecting the icons at the top of the left pane, as shown in the following image:

Regardless of where you have navigated to in the console, these icons are always available. To the left of them is a drop-down menu that provides links to recently visited areas and objects that you have looked at.

Let's now take a look at the five main areas, or locations, that you can navigate to.

Home screen

Clicking on the **Home** icon takes you to your Home screen. Home is where you find all your dashboards, and by default it displays the **Recommendations** dashboard.

There are many out-of-the-box dashboards available for you to use, and if you have the Advanced or Enterprise edition of vRealize Operations, you have the ability to create your own **Custom** dashboards. We will cover dashboards in more detail later in this chapter.

Alerts

Navigating to **Alerts** will bring up a list of all the alerts triggered by vRealize Operations. In a large environment, the list of alerts can be very long, so there are two options provided to help you filter them:

- **Filter drop-down**: This drop-down menu has a list of all the Alert fields. Selecting a field from the list opens a dialogue box where you can enter part or all of the values of the field that you want to filter. For example, if I were just looking for alerts triggered on *esx-host1*, I would select **Triggered On** from the drop-down list and enter **esx-host1** as my filter.

- **Quick Filter**: Entering text in this field filters the Alert field. For example, entering *hardening* in the quick filter box will filter the Alert list to only show the alerts with the word *hardening* in their title.

The filters you select are shown in the alerts bar and can be removed by clicking on the red X icons. In the following example, I have filtered for all the **Active** alerts with the word **hardening** in them:

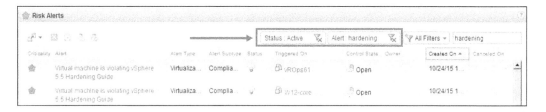

Clicking on an alert will bring up a new screen with the alert's details. Alerts are also available in a number of other places. For example, when looking at individual objects in vRealize Operations, if they have active alerts, they will be shown on the object's **Summary**, **Alerts** and **Troubleshooting** tabs.

We will cover Alerts in full in *Chapter 5, Alerts, Symptoms, Recommendations, and Actions*.

Environment

Clicking on **Environment** will bring you to a structured list of all the environments and objects that vRealize Operations is managing. This is one of the main places you will go to in order to navigate to a particular **Object Tree**.

In Environment, the left pane gives you access to your managed objects in a hierarchical manner. There are two sections:

Groups and applications

We looked at Custom Groups earlier, in *Chapter 2, Install, Configure, and Administer vRealize Operations Manager*. Clicking on **Custom Groups** here will change the pane to a list of all the Group Types available. If you click on the arrow next to each Group Type, you can view all the created groups of that particular Group Type.

Selecting a particular group will bring up the group's dashboard in the right pane.

Applications are an alternative way of creating groups of objects. They are used when you are building up more complex sets of objects to create a view of application or services. They differ from Custom Groups in two main ways:

- You can't create a rule to include group members, so group membership cannot be dynamic. All members must be manually added or removed.

- The members can be grouped into sub-groups within the construct to represent tiers within a service or application.

I tend to use Custom Group constructs by default as they offer the dynamic membership functionality and so are more flexible.

Custom Datacenters: This is a new object type introduced in vRealize Operations 6.1. It allows us to group together vCenter Servers, Datacenters, Cluster Compute Resources, and Host Systems for capacity analytics purposes.

vRealize Operations undertakes full capacity analysis of the Custom Datacenters and, in conjunction with the Workload Balancing alerts, can make recommendations on workload placement, based on the Workload Placement rules defined in our Policy.

The typical use case is where we have 2 or more Clusters, potentially on multiple vCenters, where we run our production workload. Custom Datacenters and Workload Balancing alerts help us make decisions to balance that workload across those constructs.

Inventory Trees

The **Inventory Trees** are created by the Solutions that we install and configure in vRealize Operations. Out of the box, the vSphere and End Point Operations solutions are installed, so will see the following Inventory Trees:

- **Operating Systems**: This contains a hierarchical view of our operating systems when we configure **End Point Operations** and install the agents. We will look at End Point Operations in depth in *Chapter 10, End Point Operations*.

- **Remote Checks**: Part of End Point Operations, these allow us to do a check and alert on the ICMP TCP or HTTP response against the remote systems.

- **vRealize Operations Clusters**: It is a view of the vRealize Operations solution itself.

- **vSphere Hosts and Clusters**: This hierarchical view represents the Hosts and Cluster hierarchy we have configured in our vCenter(s). It is the Inventory Tree we are likely to use the most.

- **vSphere Networking**: It is a networking-centric view of the objects, so we can see the relationships and status of the virtual switches and the port groups and so on.

- **vSphere Storage**: It is a storage-centric view of the objects.

- **All Objects**: As the title suggests, this is a list of all the objects. They are grouped first by Solution and then by object type.

As we install other Solutions and Management Packs, which we will discuss in *Chapter 7, vRealize Operations Manager Solutions*, more Inventory Trees will be created.

The Inventory Trees are very simple and intuitive to traverse. The right hand pane is context-sensitive, so as you select the objects in the tree, the dashboard or the object details screen for that object will be shown in the right pane.

In a similar way, as the right hand pane is context-sensitive, when you click on **Environment Overview** for the first time, its context is Environment Overview. It will show tabs for **Groups**, **Customer Datacenters**, **Applications,** and **Inventory**. The tabs are used as follows:

- **Groups**: This is a list of all the custom groups. Alongside the group name, it shows the current Health, Risk, and Efficiency badges. If you hover over these badges, you have the option to display their spark lines to show the recent history of the badge.

- **Custom Datacenters**: This is a list of your Custom Datacenters along with their Health, Risk, and Efficiency badges.

- **Applications**: This is a list of your Applications, along with their Health, Risk, and Efficiency badges.

- **Inventory**: Unlike Inventory Trees, this is not a hierarchical list. This is a list of all the objects in vRealize Operations, again, with their current Health, Risk, and Efficiency badges shown.

  You are likely to have many objects, so the **filter** box on the right hand side allows you to filter the list. Entering the name, or part of the name of the object in the filter box will filter the list to only the objects with that text.

In the following example, I have filtered for the objects with vRealize Operations in their name:

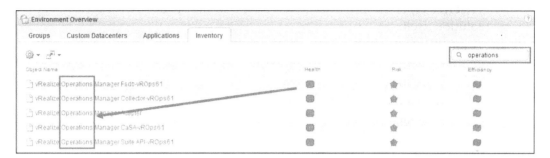

Content

This is the part of vRealize Operations where all the intellectual property, from both the Solutions you install and customizations that you make, is kept.

Details of how to use, customize, and create most of the **Content** will be covered in the subsequent chapters in this book as follows:

Chapter 3: Dashboards

Chapter 4: Views and Reports

Chapter 5: Alert Definitions, Symptom Definitions, Actions, Recommendations, and Notifications

The rest of the content can be described as follows:

- **Custom Profile**: A Custom Profile defines the custom size of an object. It is used in the **Capacity Remaining** dashboard to show how many objects of that size can fit in the remaining capacity of a container object.

- **Plugins**: These are the plugins used and installed by **End Point Operations**. We will look at End Point Operations in *Chapter 10, End Point Operations*.

- **Super Metrics**: In situations where you want to alert or report on a metric that doesn't exist but can be derived, Super Metrics can be created and used.

    A Super Metric is created out of one or more existing metrics that are collected with operands applied. You use policies to apply Super Metrics to the objects that you are monitoring.

- **Group Types**: This is where you manage the Group types for your Custom Groups. These can be thought of as folders that you put your Custom Groups in.

- **Manage Metric Config**: This is where you can create XML code to refine how some of the widgets in the custom dashboards operate.

- **Icons**: This is where you can customize the icons that will be displayed for all the object types in vRealize Operations.

Administration

Most of your administrative tasks are carried out here. We covered the Administration Panel at the end of *Chapter 2, Install, Configure and, Administer vRealize Operations Manager.*

Object search

As well as using the navigation buttons and trees, you can do a simple search for an object you are looking for. In the following screenshot, I was looking for my vRealize Operations Cluster:

1. I first entered **vROps** into the search box. This gave me a list of objects with **vROps** somewhere in their title. I selected **vROps Cluster Node 1**.

2. On selecting this, my context was changed to **vRops Cluster Node 1**. You can also see that it is easy to navigate to its **Related Hierarchies** and **Related Objects**.

3. Note that the dashboard context changed to **vROps Cluster Node 1**.

Dashboards overview

Most of the information in vRealize Operations is displayed back to you via **Dashboards**. There are three main types of dashboards that should be considered:

- **Management Pack Dashboard**: When you install Management Packs, they generally come with one or more dashboards. These are designed to visualize the objects being managed by the Management Packs, in the most effective way possible.

  These dashboards are constructed using widgets and can be readily modified to meet your specific requirements.

- **Custom Dashboards**: These are dashboards created by vRealize Operations users. These are usually created from scratch; however, it is also common to, say, clone a Management Pack dashboard and use it as a starting point for a new dashboard that you may want to create.

- **Object Details**: Whenever you select an object and go to its object details screen, you can consider it to be a dashboard for that specific object. This dashboard has a number of tabs for managing each object. These will be discussed in detail later in this chapter.

All the Management Pack and Custom dashboards are accessible via the **Home** page.

Recommendations dashboard

When you select the Home page, you will be presented with the currently configured **Default dashboard**. Out of the box, this is the **Recommendations dashboard**.

With the launch of vRealize Operations, a big change came about in the alerting and troubleshooting side of the solution, mainly in the areas of **Content** and the **alerting framework**.

The Recommendations dashboard reflects the importance of Content and the alerting framework. These capabilities come together as follows:

- **Content** comes with the Solutions and Management Packs. It is created to provide relevant and actionable alerts, based on the management best practice for the objects being managed by the Solution. It also includes intellectual property from the Content writer – this is from where much of the value of the Solution or the Management Pack can be derived.

- **Alert** Content is formed of Symptoms, Recommendations, and Actions Content, and is consumed by the alerting framework to create alerts.

- When these alerts are triggered, they immediately appear in their rank order on the Recommendations dashboard.

As a consultant with VMware, I have carried out numerous Proof of Concepts with clients, standing vRealize Operations up against their environments. I have been genuinely amazed at how quickly the solutions have zeroed in and described immediate problems in their environments. The Recommendations dashboard has been the first place where these have surfaced.

The **Recommendations** dashboard has three sections for each of the **Health**, **Risk**, and **Efficiency** badges:

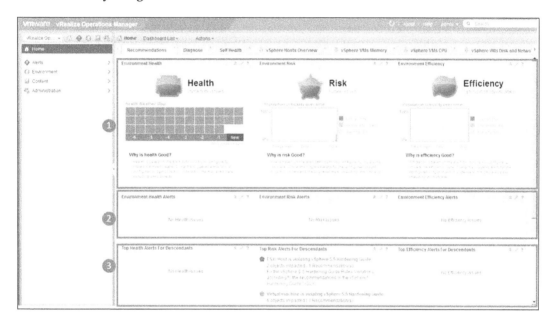

1. The top section shows the status of **Health**, **Risk,** and **Efficiency** for your entire environment.

   You will see a grid below the **Health** badge. This is a **Health Weather Map** view of the health for the entire environment over the previous 6 hours. Each box represents one object and you can view how the health of your objects has changed over the previous 6 hours by clicking on the numbers below the weather map.

   Hovering over a box will give you information on the box's identity and its Health badge and sub-badge scores. Double clicking on it will take you to the object's details screen.

2. The middle section is for alerts for the **Environment** itself.

3. The bottom section is where you will find the ranked alerts for all the descendants of the environment. As this represents your entire infrastructure, these are effectively the most important alerts, or issues, in your environment.

   Clicking on an **Alert** will take you to the Alert details screen where you can troubleshoot the issue. We will cover Alerts in greater detail in *Chapter 5, Alerts, Symptoms, Recommendations, and Actions.*

Before we look further into dashboards, we should first understand more about badges in vRealize Operations.

Badges

vRealize Operations describes the state of your infrastructure using **Badges**.

Every object has the three major badges of **Health, Risk,** and **Efficiency** calculated for them.

Every object can also have minor badges; however, not all of these badges are created or calculated for every object type. It is the job of the Solution or Management Pack to decide whether the badge is calculated and to describe how it is calculated.

For example, the **Capacity Remaining** badge for a storage object may be calculated based on the percentage remaining storage (GB), whereas for a Cluster object it needs to be based on a combination of CPU, memory, storage, and network.

The vSphere solution has all badges calculated for all object types. It will be some of the Management Packs that do not have all badges calculated. This is usually because it is just not possible or does not make sense.

For example, consider a region object type within the **Amazon Web Services (AWS)** Management Pack.

The Health badge can be calculated based on the availability metric; however, there is no concept of the capacity of a region when it comes to a consumer of AWS, so the capacity is not measured and that badge is disabled.

Health badge

This badge is used to describe any immediate issues that may exist with an object. If the status of the health badge deteriorates then it is likely that there is some immediate troubleshooting required. There are three minor badges related to health:

- **Workload**: This is a measure of the percentage of resources an object is demanding. If the object is demanding multiple resources then it is calculated based on the most constrained resource.

  For example, a Virtual Machine can have CPU, memory, disk, and network resources. The most highly demanded of these resources would determine the Workload badge score.

- **Anomalies**: This is determined by the number of metrics for the object that are outside their normal range, as determined by the **Dynamic Thresholding (DT)** analytics described in *Chapter 1*, *Introduction to vRealize Operations Manager*.

  If an object has descendant objects then the quantity of anomalies of those objects is included in the calculation.

- **Faults**: These are issues such as loss of NIC redundancy, HA issues, or hardware faults such as degraded memory. The fault score is determined by the severity of the fault(s) reported.

Risk badge

This badge is used to inform the administrator of potential future issues with an object. This is principally in the areas of **capacity** and **compliance**. If an object is projected to be running out of capacity or if it is experiencing configuration drift away from desired state, the Risk badge's value will deteriorate.

There are four minor badges related to Risk:

- **Time Remaining**: This is a calculation of how long there is before the object runs out of capacity.

- **Capacity Remaining**: This is a measure of how much capacity an object has remaining.

- **Stress**: This is a measure of how long the workload exceeds a given stress level, usually 70%, over a given period. The following screenshot is how vRealize Operations describes Stress graphically:

- **Compliance**: This is a measure of how compliant an object is with the configuration standard(s) it has been associated with.

  vSphere Hardening guidelines alerts can drive this badge; however, you can create your own configuration standard alerts to reflect your own infrastructure standards if you wish.

  If you have vRealize Advanced or Enterprise editions, you can use the integration of vCenter Configuration Manager to drive the results of this badge.

We will cover vSphere Hardening guidelines alerts in *Chapter 5, Alerts, Symptoms, Recommendations, and Actions*, and will cover Time Remaining and Capacity Remaining in more depth in *Chapter 6, Capacity Planning and Capacity Projects*.

Efficiency badge

The final badge to consider is the **Efficiency badge**, which, as the name implies, describes the level of efficiency of a given object. This shows you areas in your infrastructure where you can, perhaps, reclaim wasted resources or drive up utilization.

The Efficiency badge has two minor badges associated with it:

- **Reclaimable capacity**: This is a measure of the amount of resources that can be reclaimed. It is measured as a percentage of the provisioned capacity.
- **Density**: This describes the level of density that can be achieved if your resources are used optimally.

 If you install vRealize Operations against a traditional vSphere environment that has evolved over time, you will often see a lot of inefficiency. This is generally due to outdated capacity and operational practices. vRealize Operations helps you improve your practices and drive up efficiencies.

Badge state

The state of the Health, Risk, and Efficiency badges for a given object is determined by the active alerts for that object and the criticality of the active alerts:

- **Critical alert**: Badge will turn red
- **Immediate alert**: Badge will turn orange
- **Warning alert**: Badge will turn yellow
- **Information alert**: Badge will stay green

If an object has multiple alerts, the badge color will reflect the alert with the highest criticality.

The color of the minor badges depends on the score of the particular badge. The levels at which the badges change color are defined in Base Settings. This means they are changeable through application of Policies.

I generally find the default levels that are set are appropriate.

Now that we understand what the badges are, and what they represent, let's look at the other dashboards that are available.

Object Details dashboard

When you select an object in vRealize Operations, you are generally taken to its **Object Details** dashboard. How you navigate there depends on where you are. Sometimes you double click on an object, sometimes you highlight it, and sometimes you click on an **Object Details** icon to navigate to it.

As you can see in the following screenshot, the **Object Details** dashboard is comprised of a number of tabs through which you manage the object:

Summary tab

This tab is, in effect, a **Recommendations** dashboard for the object in question. It shows the current state of Health, Risk, and Efficiency. These badges are based on the active alerts for the object, which are displayed in the middle section.

The bottom section, just like the Recommendations dashboard, shows the alerts for the descendant objects.

As can be seen in the previous dashboard for host **esx-01a.copr.local**, Risk is critical as there is a critical alert for the object – **ESXi Host is violating vSphere 5.5 Hardening Guide**. If I were to click on the link, it would tell me exactly what was wrong by taking me to the alert.

Alerts

Clicking on the **Alerts** tab brings up a list of all the alerts for the object.

You interact with the **Alerts** tab as follows:

1. The same **filter** options that we saw earlier in this chapter with the Alerts dashboard can be used here. In the preceding case, I have filtered only on the **Active** alerts.

2. The Alert tab Toolbar has the following capabilities, from left to right:

   ° **Open in external application**: This opens the selected object in an external application. For example, in the preceding case, it would allow me to open the ESXi host in the vSphere Web Client.

   ° **Cancel Alert**: This is typically used for Fault or Event alerts. Once you have resolved the problem, you should cancel the alert.

   ° **Suspend Alert**: This stops the alert affecting the object badges while you are working on the problem.

   ° **Take Ownership**: This allows your colleagues to know that you are aware of the alert problem and are fixing it.

   ° **Release Ownership**

   ° **Show Self Alerts**: This toggles the visibility of the object's alerts.

   ° **Show Ancestor Alerts**: This toggles visibility of all the alerts for higher level objects (parents, grandparents, and so on).

   ° **Show Descendant Alerts**: This toggles visibility of all the alerts for lower level objects (children, grandchildren, and so on).

3. To look at the alert's details, click on the alert itself.

We will look at alerts in depth, including Alert details, in *Chapter 5, Alerts, Symptoms, Recommendations, and Actions*.

Analysis

The analysis tab is where you find details about all the minor badges. This tab itself has tabs representing each of the minor badges for that object. The minor badges will be colored in these tabs to represent their state.

If you have been alerted to an issue related to a badge score, this is where you should come in order to see more details about the particular badge.

We will look at the **Compliance** tab in *Chapter 5*, *Alerts, Symptoms, Recommendations, and Actions* and capacity-related tabs in *Chapter 6*, *Capacity Planning and Capacity Projects*.

Troubleshooting

This is where you should go, as you would expect, to help troubleshoot the issues with a given object. There are four additional tabs within the **Troubleshooting** tab:

Symptoms

This is a list of all the **Symptoms** for an object that are currently triggered. It gives you an at a glance view of everything that could be impacting the object with spark lines for key information. The columns are all sortable by clicking on the column headings.

Timeline

The Timeline is a very rich interface for viewing Symptoms, Alerts, and Events.

There are two main areas you interact with in this dashboard:

1. **Staggered timeline**: This shows a view of the selected **Symptoms, Alerts,** and **Events** over three different time ranges, representing short, medium, and long periods of historical time. In the preceding screenshot, you can see that the top area covers the previous 2 hours, the middle area covers the previous 2 days, and the bottom area covers the previous 2 weeks.

   Each Symptom, Alert, or Event is represented by a colored line and the color of the line represents its severity.

   You can use your mouse to drag the time window to the beginning of event lines and hover over them to have more details pop up.

2. **Toolbar options**: You make selections in the toolbar to change the objects being shown in the timeline. From left to right:

   ○ **Impact**: Choose whether you want to see the items with a Health, Risk, or Efficiency impact. In the preceding screenshot, all three are selected.

   ○ **Show Symptoms**: If selected, all symptoms for the object(s) are shown.

- ° **Events**: If you select this, a drop-down menu is made available to select the type of events to include in the view.

- ° **Select Status**: Helps you choose whether you want to see active and/or cancelled events.

- ° **Select Criticality of Events**: You choose the criticality of the events to be displayed. For example, you may only be interested in the Critical events.

- ° **Show Self Events**: Toggles visibility of events for the selected object.

- ° **Show Ancestor and Descendant Events**: Often it is useful to layer on the events from the parent or child objects. These two drop-down menus allow you to select the ancestor or descendant object types to include in the view.

- ° **Show peer events**: This shows all the object's peer events. For example, if it were a host, it would show all the events for the other hosts in the cluster.

- ° **Date Range**: This helps you select the date range you are interested in.

Events

The **Events** tab is similar to the Timeline. However, along with being able to choose the set of object events to view, you can also overlay them onto a metric line of one of your badges.

All Metrics

This is my favorite tab in Troubleshooting and I spend a lot of time here. It allows us to see the status of the related objects in a very simple way. At the same time, you can drill down into the minutest of detail using the metric selector and metric graph window.

You interact with All Metrics as follows:

1. **Relationship Map**: Here you can see the related objects of the object you are troubleshooting.

2. **Metric Selector**: This is a hierarchical list of all the metrics associated with the object selected in the Relationship Map. If you click on a different object in the map, this will change to reflect the metrics available for the new object you have selected.

Notice the filter box: With hundreds of metrics potentially available for each object, you can enter text in the filter box to help you find the metric you are looking for. For example, if you enter demand in the box, it will filter the hierarchical tree to only include the metrics with demand in their name.

3. **Metric Graph**: If you double-click on a metric in the Metric Selector, it will be displayed as a graph in the right hand window.

    There are a variety of options available in this graph view to change such things as how you want to view the *X* and *Y* axes, whether you want to add the trend lines, and whether you would like the graphs stacked. You can also change the date range of the graphs here.

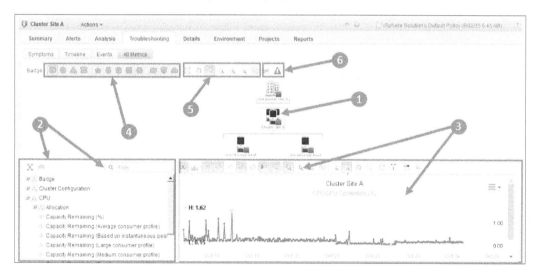

4. **Badge**: The objects in the Relationship Map have a colored icon next to them representing their badge state. You change the badge this is based on by using the badge selector.

5. **Relationship Map view options**: The map can get quite large and busy for some objects. Here you can zoom it in or out, pan, and reset to initial view.

6. **Object Details** and **Alerts**: These two icons allow you to jump straight to the Object Details or alerts dashboards of the object selected in the map.

Details

The **Details** tab is another area in vRealize Operations that showcases the Content that has been created by the Solutions and Management Packs. There are two tabs within **Details**:

- **Views**: We use Views in vRealize Operations to display the underlying data in a meaningful way. As well as being used in this tab, Views are also used in **Custom Dashboards** and in **Reports**. We will cover Views in detail in *Chapter 4*, *Views and Reports*.

- **Heatmaps**: Here we can visualize two metrics for a set of objects. The first metric dictates the size of the objects in the heatmap and the second metric dictates the color. The purpose is to highlight the important objects with potential problems.

  When describing the capability to clients, I usually say *With heatmaps, you just need to look for the big red thing!*. This is shown in the following example, which shows all the datastores sized by usage and colored by latency.

Environment

This is sometimes called the **Skittle view**. It is a hierarchical view of all the objects relevant to the selected object, showing their current badge statuses.

You can select the badge you want to view at the top of the screen, as well as change the order of display and the badge colors you want to see. For a very large infrastructure, this is useful – you may not want to see the *green* objects, preferring just to focus in on the problem objects.

If you select an object in the tree, all the objects that are not related to it are dimmed. This allows you to easily see the status of related objects.

Projects

The projects tab is used by Capacity Projects. We will look at these in *Chapter 6, Capacity Planning and Capacity Projects*.

Reports

The **Reports** tab shows all the reports that can be run against the selected object. We will cover Reports in *Chapter 4, Views and Reports*.

Out-of-the-box and Custom dashboards

We have covered the Object Details dashboard and you will have seen that these are not customizable at all.

The other dashboards that you will use and create are all very customizable and we will cover these in this section.

To a large extent, the dashboards that you get out-of-the-box and the ones that are installed by Solutions and Management Packs are the same as the custom dashboards you will create yourself. The only difference is that they have been created by someone else.

Anatomy of a Custom dashboard

The purpose of **Custom dashboards** in vRealize Operations is to visualize information about your infrastructure in ways that are intuitive, relevant, and meaningful to you. A dashboard is a relatively straightforward construct, made up of:

- **Layout**: One or more columns of varying widths.
- **Widgets**: These are the elements that make up the dashboard. They vary from lists of objects to more complicated widgets such as heatmaps.
- **Interactions**: In dashboards, you will commonly see widgets interact with each other. For example, you may select an object in one widget that will drive the context and behavior of another widget.
- **Context**: A widget needs context which defines the object(s) it is displaying or its starting configuration.

  Widgets can either be **Self Providers**, in which case you configure the widget directly with the context you want, or they can have their context configured by a **Provider** widget, defined in **Interactions**.

For example, the Object Relationship widget, configured as a **Self Provider**, could have your main vCenter as its initial context. When you open the dashboard, you will see your vCenter in the middle with all its relationships.

Alternatively, you could have another widget, such as the **Top-N widget**, listing all of your hosts. This could act as the Provider for the Object Relationship widget. When you click on a host in the Top-N widget, the context of the Object Relationship changes, focusing on the host you have selected.

- **Users and Permissions:** Once the dashboard is built, it needs to be assigned to users.

vSphere Solution dashboards

When you install vRealize Operations, the first Solution you install is the **vSphere Solution**. This installs 10 dashboards for you to use immediately.

To access the dashboards, navigate to **Home** and in the **Dashboard List** select **vSphere Dashboards**:

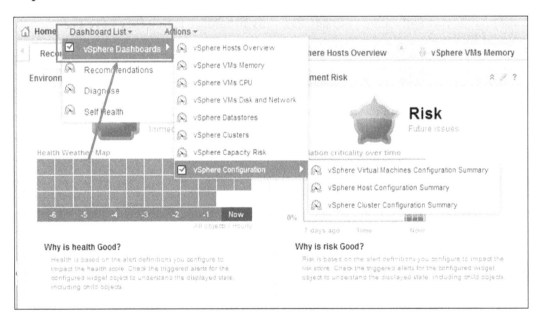

The dashboards that are available to you are:

- **vSphere Hosts Overview**
- **vSphere VMs Memory**
- **vSphere VMs CPU**
- **vSphere VMs Disk and Network**
- **vSphere Datastores**
- **vSphere Clusters**
- **vSphere Capacity Risk**
- **vSphere Virtual Machines Configuration Summary**
- **vSphere Host Configuration Summary**
- **vSphere Cluster Machines Configuration Summary**

The following is a screenshot of the **vSphere VMs CPU** dashboard, which is typical of the Out of the Box vSphere dashboards.

It uses two of the key dashboard widgets:

- **Heatmaps**: You will see that there are four heat maps. They are all colored by a key memory metric and sized by memory demand. The principle here is to highlight the busiest VMs which are suffering from key indicators of performance issues.

  If you have a VM with low memory demand then it will generally be of less interest to you than VMs that are running more workload.

- **Top 25s**: The Top-N widget is a great widget! In this example, it is listing the top 25 VMs, as measured by memory Demand and memory swap.

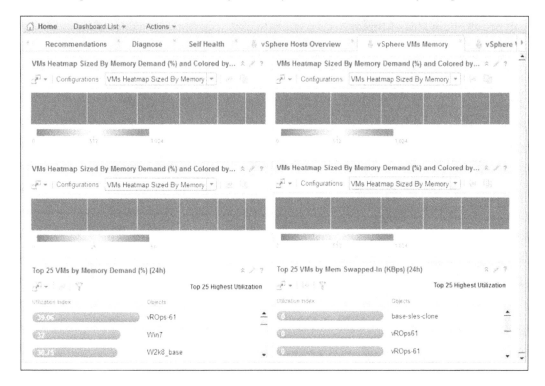

Widgets

The key to a great dashboard is taking advantage of the 44 **Widgets** available to you in vRealize Operations.

The following is a list of some of the most commonly used widgets and how you would generally use them.

Selection widgets

This first section can be considered *top level* or selection widgets. If you are using **widget interactions**, these will be your **Provider** widgets that will determine the context of the other widgets.

- **Health Chart**: This widget displays a metric, usually health but it can be any metric, over a period of time as a rolling chart. It's very useful for spotting trends and providing the overall status of a set of objects. It could sometimes be used as a main display in an Operations Center.

- **Top-N**: This is a great widget for listing the top offenders of a given metric. For example, you could list the top 25 datastores based on a latency metric. This will highlight the datastores more likely to be needing attention.

  Using interactions, you could link the widget to a second Top-N widget, listing the child VMs of the selected datastore, and their latency or other disk usage metric. Using the two together in this way, you would see the troublesome datastores and then the VMs likely causing or being impacted by the problems.

- **Object Relationship**: This is the same widget that is in the **Troubleshooting | All Metrics** tab in the Object Details dashboard. It works both as a starting widget, highlighting a particular area that you want to click through for more detail, and as a widget being provided its context by another widget.

- **Environment Overview**: This is a customizable version of the Environment tab in the Object Details dashboard. You can set it to display all the objects or limit the view to certain specific Object Types and/or objects.

  It can even be customized to show different metric data.

- **Metric Picker**: This is most commonly used in conjunction with the Metric Chart widget. I would usually have the Metric Picker widget provided its context by one of the above selection widgets. The Metric Picker widget would then be the Provider to the Metric Chart widget.

Visualization widgets

Visualization widgets allow the administrator to see information and problems in very appealing and intuitive ways. The main widgets used for visualization are:

- **Heatmap**: This is probably my favorite widget. It shows the object's metrics in two dimensions:

    ◦ **Size**: The size of the block in the heatmap is relative to the value of the metric.

    ◦ **Color**: The color of the block in the heatmap is relative to the value of the metric. The scale of the coloring can optionally be tuned to affect best practice. For example, in a heatmap where color is used for disk latency, you may decide that you want the objects to be colored green until they reach the point at which latency is an issue – perhaps 20ms. You may then say that between 20ms and 30ms, you want the color to graduate toward red, and over 30ms the color should be simply red.

- **Metric Chart**: This widget shows the value of a metric over a period of time. You can customize the metric in various ways, including showing a specific period of time, a trend line, and the dynamic thresholds calculated for the time frame you are looking at.

  The Metric Chart can also be 'stacked' – this allows you to see the value of a particular metric over, say, the period of a week, overlayed with the value of that same metric over the previous week.

- **Weather Map**: Similar to weather maps that show the movement of rain over a region, weather maps in vRealize Operations show how a given metric, for example, object health, has changed over a period of time for a range of objects. It gives the viewer real insight into how and where something like Health is varying or degrading.

- **Scoreboard**: This is probably the most used widget within an Operations Center. It shows one or more metrics with a traffic light color to determine the state of an object. In a Network Operations Center, that may be the state of their datacentre or a particular application that is important to an organization

- **Capacity Utilization**: New to vRealize Operations 6.1, this widget helps visualize the relative utilization of the descendant objects of a given container. For example, for a Cluster Compute Resource, it can show the relative capacity utilization of related host systems, VMs, and datastores. It shows under-utilized resources to the left and over-utilized resources to the right.

The View widget

New to vRealize Operations 6 is the **View Widget**. This widget allows the user to see the results of a View within the dashboard context.

We will cover Views in detail in the next chapter. Views allow you to see an extract of any set of metrics or properties for any set of objects in an extremely customizable way. Views can also be repurposed into Reports that can be created and circulated as needed.

Views will become an increasingly important part of vRealize Operations as the solution matures further.

Other widgets

The widgets discussed so far are the main widgets used in vRealize Operations. However, there are many other widgets that can be used to build up a dashboard.

The best way to explore the various widgets available to you is to explore the **Create Dashboard** option within Content.

Exploring the New Custom Dashboard workspace

To explore the **New Custom dashboard Workspace**, refer to the following figure:

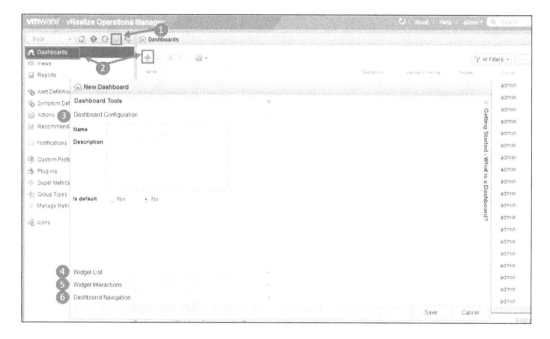

1. Click on the Content icon.
2. Select **Dashboard** and click on the Plus icon to create a dashboard.

   In the **New Dashboard** workspace, complete the following sections:

3. **Dashboard Configuration**: You have the following options:
   - **Name**
   - **Description**
   - **Is Default**: If you select this, then the dashboard becomes your default dashboard on your Home page.

4. **Widget List**: The widgets, in the left hand pane, can be dragged into the canvas on the right. Once you have dragged in the widgets, you can configure them by clicking on the pencil icon in the upper right hand corner of the widget.

   Every widget has different configuration options — click on the Help icon to see the details of exactly how to configure each widget.

5. **Widget Interactions**: This is where you define which widgets are **Provider** widgets, providing context for the receiving widgets.

 When you create an interaction, always make sure you click on the **Apply Interactions** button in the box. If you move onto the next step before doing so, the interactions will not be saved.

6. **Dashboard Navigation**: With Dashboard Navigation, you can use the widgets in the dashboard you are creating as the Provider widgets to the widgets in the other dashboards. This allows you to create a workflow for more advanced troubleshooting dashboards.

7. Once you have completed all the sections in the Create Dashboard workspace, click on **Save** to complete building your first dashboard.

Summary

In this chapter, we covered the main User Interface for interacting with vRealize Operations.

You were introduced to the Recommendations Dashboard, which I believe is always a great first place to go to, and the Object Details dashboard, which you will use to troubleshoot, manage, and assess the capacity of your infrastructure.

We looked at badges and how the major and minor badges are used to describe our environment.

Finally, we looked at custom dashboards and the widgets that are available to us to build dashboards to meet our operational imperatives.

In the next chapter, we are going to start drilling into how we can build up Views and Reports.

4
Views and Reports

In this chapter, we are going to look at how you can visualize the objects, properties, and data within vRealize Operations using Views.

We will show you how the Views can be combined to create compelling Reports, and also how they can be added to Dashboards.

Finally, we will look at some of the key built-in Report templates, which come with vRealize Operations, and how you can use the reporting engine to schedule the regular creation and distribution of Reports.

An overview of Views and Reports

In the previous versions of vRealize Operations, formally called vCenter Operations, the reporting capability was very limited. There were some good out-of-the-box reports in the vSphere UI; however, they were not easily customizable and the Custom UI had no reporting available at all.

With the release of vRealize Operations, this has been transformed, with the addition of the following three new capabilities:

- **Views**: A View is the visualization of information held in vRealize Operations. It can take a number of forms or **Presentations**, such as a Table, List, or Pie Chart, to show the information in the way you want it to be shown.

- **Reports**: The views that you create can be incorporated into Reports. A Report is how you get information out of vRealize Operations. It is, in essence, a set of views that are exported in the .PDF or .CSV format. Reports can be run on an ad hoc basis, or they can be scheduled.

- **Dashboards**: We covered Dashboards in *Chapter 3*, *Dashboards, Badges, and Widgets*. The important new capability in vRealize Operations 6.1 is that Views can also be reused as Dashboard content. In the Object Details dashboards, the **Details** tab lists the available Views for that object.

In this chapter, we will look at these constructs in more detail. Let's start by creating some Views that we will use later to build a Report.

Views

As mentioned earlier, Views are used to display data from vRealize Operations in order to help administrators understand and interpret the information available to them. There are five parts that make up a View:

- **Name** and **Description** of the View.
- **Presentation** is how the View is going to be displayed. For example, it could be a Table of objects, and their metrics or properties, or it could be a distribution of specific objects, metrics, or properties in the form of a pie chart.

  We will look at all six Presentation types:

- **Subject**: This is the object type(s) that the View is going to be based on
- **Data**: This is the data regarding those object types, that we are going to expose, and visualize in the View
- **Visibility**: The areas in vRealize Operations that the View is going to be available in.

The foundations of compelling Views and Reports are built on how you use the Presentation types to display data in a meaningful way.

Building Custom Views

In this section, we will build some custom Views using some of the main **Presentation** types available to you in the View workspace.

The List View

These are probably the most used presentation type, and are the easiest way to get structured information, and data, out of vRealize Operations.

For our first View, let's create a **List** View of all the virtual machines in your environment, with key information about how they are configured:

1. First, navigate to **Content**, then **Views**.

2. Click on the *plus* icon to add a new View. This will bring up the **Create new View** workspace.

3. In the first part of the workspace, you need to give the View a **Name** and **Description**, for example **My Virtual Machine List with Snapshots**, and then some descriptive text on what the View is designed to show.

4. Click on **2. Presentation**.

5. Clicking on **List**, will select the **Presentation** type, and start populating a review of the View on the right-hand side of the workspace.

   Some of the Presentation types have **configuration** options; in the case of List, you have the option to show how many listed items are to be shown on each page.

6. Next, we need to select the **Object Type** that this View is designed for. Click on **3. Subjects**, and then, in the **Select a Subject** dropdown, click on the arrow next to **vCenter Adapter**.

   Now scroll down to find and select the **Virtual Machine** object type.

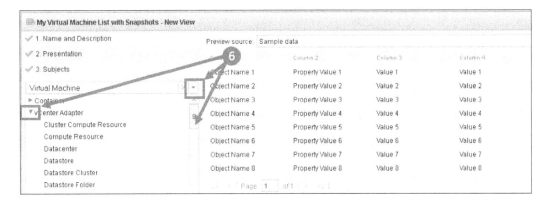

7. Next, click on **4. Data**, so we can start selecting the data that we want in the List.

    Finding the exact metric can sometimes be a bit hit and miss, as their names don't always reflect exactly what you are looking for. You will find details on what each metric is in the *vRealize Operations Manager Customization and Administration Guide*, which is available from the VMware website.

8. We now need to find the **metrics** or **properties** we are interested in. Expand the **CPU** part of the metric tree and locate the **Current Size in Unit(s)** metric. Drag that metric into the data section of the workspace, to add it to your View.

9. We can customize how the data field is displayed. As you can see in the following screenshot, I have changed the Metric Label to **vCPUs** as it is a more descriptive name than **Current Size in Unit(s)**:

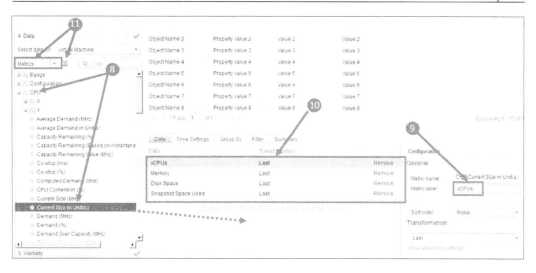

10. Now, we need to drag three more metric fields to the Data list. Either traverse the metric tree, or search for the metrics using the Filter box above the metric tree. The metrics we want to add are:

    ° **Memory | Guest Configured Memory (KB)**. Change the label to **Memory**. In the configuration section for this metric, you could, optionally, change the units to **GB**, instead of **KB**.

    ° **Guest File System stats | Total Guest File System Capacity (GB)**. Change the label to **Disk Space**.

    ° **Disk Space | Snapshot Space (GB)**. Change the label to **Snapshot Space Used**.

11. One thing to note is the **Show Metrics/Property** dropdown. This will change the metric tree selector, to a **property** tree selector, so you can select properties for your View.

> Next to the dropdown is a **Select Object** icon. When the metric tree is enumerated, vRealize Operations takes a random selection of five objects and discovers all the metrics and properties for those objects. It uses these to populate the trees.
>
> Sometimes, it might pick objects that don't have the particular metric or property, for example a **Custom Tag**, you are looking for. If you encounter this, use the **Select Object** icon and you will get the metric and property trees from that object to pick from.

12. Finally, click on **5. Visibility**, to see the options available, regarding where the View can be seen, and used. In this case we will use the defaults. There is also the option to blacklist the View for certain object types.

13. Click on **Save**, to complete the creation of the View.

As you will have seen, during the creation of your first View, there are a number of other options available to you. We will cover many of these as we build some of the other Views, for your first report.

Preview source

Sometimes, it is useful to get a quick review of what the View is going to look like as you build it. This is particularly the case if you are not sure of the exact metric, or property, you are looking for.

In the **Create View** workspace, you will have seen the **Preview** pane at the top. If you click on **Preview source**, then select **vSphere World**, you will see a preview of what your View will look like.

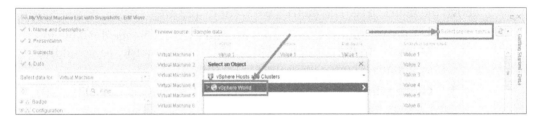

Now that you have created your first View, you can go and see what it looks like in the vRealize Operations UI.

Navigate to **Environment | vSphere Hosts and Clusters | vSphere World**, and click on the **Details** tab. In the list of Views, look for the View you just created, click on it, and the View will appear in the bottom pane.

In this case, the View will show details of all the Virtual Machines in your inventory. If you were to navigate the vSphere World tree down to a cluster and look at the View in a cluster context, it would show all the Virtual Machines in just that cluster.

The Trend View

The next view that we will look at is the **Trend View**. This will generally show **historical** and **forecast** data for one or more metrics.

In the example we will work through now, this is going to be the quantity of Hosts, and Virtual Machines, that have been running over the previous 90 days with a forecast for the upcoming 30 days.

It is intended to be a high-level snapshot, for the beginning of the report we will create later:

1. First, navigate to **Content** then **Views**.

2. Click on the **plus** icon to add a new View. This will bring up a **Create new View** workspace.

3. In the first part of the workspace, you need to give the View a **Name** and **Description**, for example, **My Running Hosts and VMs Trend View**, and then some descriptive text on what the View is designed to show.

4. Click on **2. Presentation**.

5. Clicking on **Trend** will select the Trend **Presentation** type and start populating the review of the View on the right-hand side of the workspace.

6. Next, we need to add the **Subjects** for this View, so click on **3. Subjects**.

   Unlike **Lists**, which are formed of a lot of objects and generally run against **Parent** or **Container** objects, the Trend View is based on the metrics of a single object.

   For this particular View, we might want to look at the quantity of Hosts, and Virtual Machines, not just at the vSphere World level, but also at the Virtual Center, Datacenter, or Cluster level.

   To that end, we need to explicitly state, in the Subjects section, all the object types this View is designed for.

7. As with the Lists View, in the **Select a Subject** dropdown, click on the arrow next to **vCenter Adapter**. Scroll down and select your first object type, **vSphere World**.

8. Now we need to select additional Subjects. Click on **Add Subject**, and add the following vCenter Adapter Object Types:

   ◦ **vCenter Server**

   ◦ **Datacenter**

   ◦ **Cluster Compute Resource**

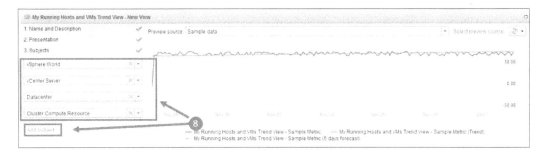

9. Now click on **4. Data**, so we can start selecting the data that we want in our Trend View.

10. We now need to find the metrics we are interested in. Expand the **Summary** part of the metric tree, and locate the **Number of Running Hosts** metric. Drag that metric into the data section of the workspace, to add it to your View.

11. Again, we can customize how the data field is displayed. In this case, as you can see in the following screenshot, I have changed the **Metric Label** to just **Hosts** to keep the View tidy.

12. Now, for this metric, we need to change some of the parameters:

    ◦ Set **Forecast Data for the next** a value of **30 Days**.

    Notice the three Data Series options. These set whether you are going to show the following in your View. For this View, we will leave all the options checked:

    ◦ **Historical Data**: Checking this box adds historical data to the View.

    ◦ **Trend of the Historical Data**: This overlays a trend line to the historical data metric line.

    ◦ **Forecast for the next 30 Days**: Checking this box adds forecasted data to the View. You can also set how far in the future you want to forecast for.

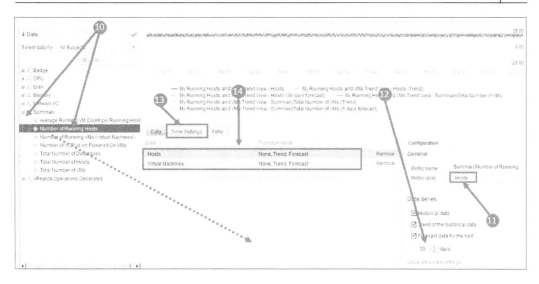

13. Next, we need to set the time frame for the historical data trend. Click on the **Time Settings** tab, change **Relative Date Range** to **Last 90 Days**, and then click on **Data** again to return to the **Data** tab.

14. Now, we need to add a second metric field, to the Data list. Drag the **Summary | Number of Running VMs (Virtual Machine(s))** into the data section of the workspace, and make the same changes to **Relative Date Range** and **Forecast data for the next** fields as you made to the preceding Hosts metric.

15. Finally, click on **5. Visibility**. This time, we will expose this View to one of the analysis tabs. Click on the **Checkbox** next to **Workload**, and click on **Save** to complete the View creation.

Now you can go and see what the impact of that final change was. Navigate to **Environment | vSphere Hosts and Clusters | vSphere World**, and click on the **Analysis | Workload** tab. You should see your new View, in the list of **Further Analysis** links on the right-hand side.

Distribution View

The next View we will look at is the **Distribution View**. This allows you to create **pie charts or bar charts** to show the distribution of a particular metric or property associated with objects in your estate.

In the example we will work though here, we will create a View that shows the status of VMware Tools, across all your Virtual Machines:

1. First, navigate to **Content** then **Views**.

2. Click on the *plus* icon to add a new View. This will bring up the **Create new View** workspace.

3. In the first part of the workspace, you need to give the View a **Name** and **Description**, for example, **My VMware Tools Version Distribution**, and then some descriptive text about what the View is designed to show.

4. Click on **2. Presentation**.

5. Clicking on **Distribution** will select the Presentation type, and start populating the review of the View, on the right-hand side of the workspace.

6. You will see that in this View, there are a number of configuration options for this Presentation type. For this sort of pie chart, where there will be discrete values, the following changes should be made:

    ◦   Change **Visualization** to **Pie chart**.

    ◦   Click on the **Discrete distribution** radio button.

    ◦   Select the **Max number of buckets** checkbox, and set **Count** to 10.

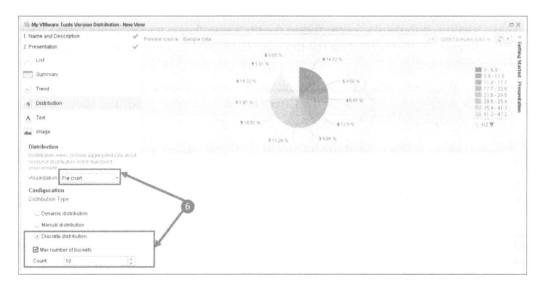

7. Next, we need to select the object type that we are designing this View for. Click on **3. Subjects**, and then in the **Select a Subject** dropdown, click on the arrow next to **vCenter Adapter**.

   Now scroll down and select the Object Type **Virtual Machine**.

8. Click on **4. Data**, so we can start selecting the data that we want in this Distribution view.

9. With this View, we are not going to display a metric, but a **property** of the Virtual Machines. We need to change the metric selector, to the property selector by changing the dropdown to **Properties**.

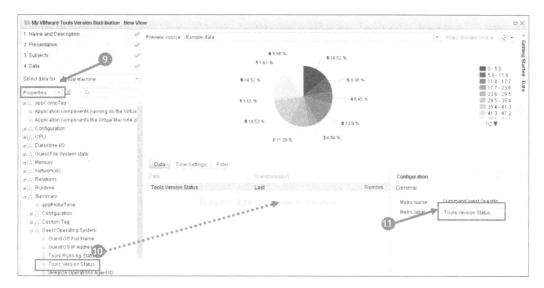

10. Navigate the property metric tree to **Summary | Guest Operating System**, and drag the **Tools Version Status** metric into the data section of the workspace, to add it to your View.

11. Again, we can customize how the data field is displayed. In this case, I have changed the Metric Label to just **Tools Version Status**, to keep the View tidy.

12. We don't need to change **5. Visibility**, so we can just click on **Save**, to complete the View creation.

To see what the View looks like, navigate to **Environment | vSphere Hosts and Clusters | vSphere World**, click on the **Details** tab, locate your View, and click on it to display the results.

Other Views

List, Trend, and Distribution Views, are the main Views that you will use on a regular basis, to customize reporting, and visualization of your environment. There are three other Views that you can use from time to time:

- **Summary View**: This shows metrics in a slightly different form to the List Views. The metrics themselves are listed and the values are aggregations of that metric across the objects that the View is focused on.

- **Text View**: This is just free form text you can insert into a report or dashboard. This is used where you might need to add just a section of text to document a report or dashboard.

- **Image View**: This final View is similar to the Text View, in that it allows you to add static images into a report or dashboard, for example, your company or departmental logo.

Refining Views

In the preceding examples, we have used many of the default settings within Views, and that will generally cater to the vast majority of the Views that you require. In some cases, however, you might want to apply a bit more refinement to the visualization.

Some of the options that weren't covered in the preceding sections are:

- **Sort Order**: In List and Summary Views, you can sort the display of metrics in ascending or descending order.

- **Transformation**: This determines how the data is displayed in the View. In most of the Views we created earlier, we just used the **Last** data point. This will display the last known or last collected value of a metric.

  There are other options that can be selected, and their values are calculated based on the **Show data for the last** *(time period)* field:

  - **Minimum**
  - **Maximum**
  - **Average**
  - **Sum**
  - **Standard Deviation**
  - **Metric Correlation**: This is very powerful. It allows you to see a given metric's value when an alternative metric is at its minimum or maximum within the time range.

○ **Forecast**

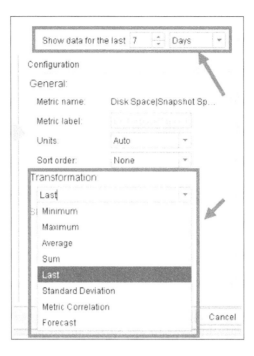

- **Series roll up**: The default is 5 minutes, however, you might decide to choose longer periods, for some Views, which might provide smoother visualizations.

- **Projects**: We will cover **Capacity Projects** in *Chapter 6, Capacity Planning and Capacity Projects*. Where the metric is relevant, you have the option to include committed Capacity Projects into the forecasted value of a given metric.

- **Filtering**: The final refinement option is to add a filter to the set of objects. This allows you to limit the set of objects that you are running the View against.

  For example, in the List View we created, we might only want to report on Production servers. We could have added a filter to the View that, say, limited the list of reported Virtual Machines based on the text **PROD** being in their machine name.

  The exact same rich criteria sets that we saw in *Chapter 2, Install, Configure, and Administer vRealize Operations Manager*, with respect to creating Groups can be used in filters.

Managing Views

As you build the set of Views you are going to use in your environment, you will find the options to **manage** your Views very useful. There are three main ways in which you manage your Views, and they can be found in **Content | Views**.

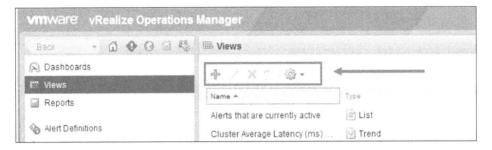

- **Create** or **Delete** Views: Use the green *plus* or red X icon, to create or delete views.

- **Clone**: Use the *Clone* icon, to make a copy of a View. This is a great way to get started with Views, or to learn more about how to create them. There are many Views provided out of the box, so if there is a View, which is close to the one you would like to create, then simply clone the view and edit the cloned version to meet your requirements.

- **Export** or **Import** Views: Click on the *cog* icon to export or import your Views as XML files. This allows you to copy Views between vRealize Operations instances.

Using Views in Dashboards

In *Chapter 3, Dashboards, Badges, and Widgets*, we looked at **Custom Dashboards**, and the **Widgets** that you can use. You can use the View Widget to add your Views to Custom Dashboards.

When you are building dashboards in the New Dashboard workspace, you drag the Widgets onto your dashboard canvas. You then click on the Pencil icon to configure the dashboard as can be seen in the following screenshot:

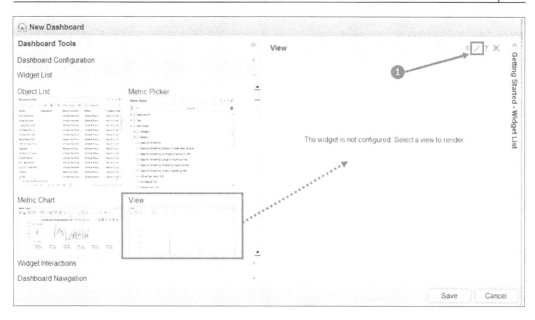

Subsequent configuration of the View widget is achieved by following these steps:

1. Once you have dragged the View Widget to your dashboard canvas, click on the **Pencil** icon to edit the View Widget.

2. Give the Widget an appropriate **Title**.

3. Use the radio buttons, to select whether the Widget is a **Self Provider** or not:

    ○ **On**: The widget is a Self Provider, so you will select the context of the Widget in the following Step 4.

    ○ **Off**: You will need to configure the **Providing Widget** in Widget Interactions, as described in *Chapter 3, Dashboards, Badges, and Widgets*.

4. If the Widget is a Self Provider, browse the vSphere World tree for the context you want to run the View against. If the Widget is not a Self Provider, this panel will be grayed out.

5. Select the **View** you want to use for the Widget. As there are a lot of Views to select from, you can use the **Filter** box to narrow your search.

    In the following example, I have used the text My to narrow the search to the Views we have created in this chapter.

6. Finally, click on **Save**, to complete the configuration.

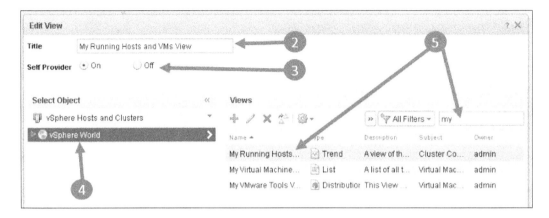

Reports

In vRealize Operations, **Reports** are the main way in which you export information. As with Views, Reports are available in **Content**. Reports have two tabs associated with them:

- **Report Templates**: These are all the Report Templates that can be run
- **Generated Reports**: This is a historical list of reports that have been run

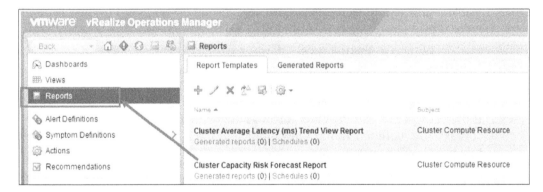

As well as being accessible in Content, Reports can also be accessed via the **Reports** tab on each object dashboard. When accessed in this way, the Report Templates and Generated Reports are contextual to the object dashboard.

For example, if you are looking at a particular Host System, you will only see Report Templates that can be run against that Host System, and the list of Generated Reports will only show Reports that have been run against that particular Host System.

Built-in Reports

When you install vRealize Operations you will get approximately 50 Report Templates, precreated for you out of the box. They can be categorized as follows:

- **Performance**: These report on how parts of your infrastructure are performing. Of particular note, are the storage focused Report Templates, which report on Latency and IOPS, for clusters and hosts.

- **Capacity**: One of the strengths of vRealize Operations is its rich Capacity Management capabilities. This is enhanced by the readymade Report Templates available to you.

- **Efficiency and Optimization**: There are a number of very useful Report Templates, which will highlight areas where you can reclaim parts of your infrastructure.

  For example, the **Idle Virtual Machines** Report Template will create a report on Virtual Machines, which barely consume any of the resources allocated to them.

  These are machines identified as idle, and they are candidates for resource reclamation. My experience in the field is that it is not uncommon to find organizations who are operating a mature virtual infrastructure having 25 percent or more of their VMs idle and candidates for reclamation.

- **Inventory**: There are a number of Report Templates that help you simply list your VMs and Hosts.

- **Configuration**: With the latest version of vRealize Operations, a huge number of VM and Host properties are now collected and stored. Some of the Report Templates take advantage of this additional data.

  For example, the **Virtual Machine Configured OS Compared to the In-Guest OS** Report Template, will create a Report that will highlight where you might have misconfigured your Virtual Hardware.

Creating and scheduling reports

Reports can either be created on an **ad hoc** basis or they can be **scheduled** for regular creation.

Creating reports on an ad hoc basis

Suppose, we want to find out which of the Virtual Machines in our environment are idle and therefore, are candidates for reclamation. To do this, we would probably run the **Idle Virtual Machines** Report Template against the vSphere World. There are two places to accomplish this:

- **Content**: All of the Report Templates are available to you in the Reports section of Content. To create a Report complete the following steps:

  1. Locate the Report Template you want to use. If you know part of the name, then enter that into the **quick filter** box.

     Alternatively, or additionally, if you are browsing the Report Templates and want to see those, for just one **Subject** type, for example, just Virtual Machines, use the **All Filters** button to select just the Subject type you are interested in.

     In the following example, you can see I have narrowed down the list to Report Templates for **Virtual Machines**, with the word **idle** in them.

  2. Click on the **Run template** icon.

     You now need to set the context of the Report. By default, the **vSphere World** context will be shown, and you can just select it and click on **OK** to run the report.

     Alternatively, traverse the vSphere Hosts and Clusters tree to find a lower level object, such as a Cluster, to run the Report Template against.

  3. Once the Report Template has run, click on **Generated Reports** to see the available Reports and to download them for viewing. Most reports are created as PDFs and CSVs.

- Object dashboard — when you are browsing an object's dashboard, you can select the **Reports** tab and run reports from there.

  The process is almost identical to the previous example, except you do not need to set a context in Step 2, as the context is, automatically, the object dashboard you are in.

Scheduling reports

As with ad hoc reports, you can schedule the running of Report Templates in both Content and object dashboards, and again, the only difference is the additional step to create the context, when you schedule the generation of reports from Content. The process is as follows:

1. Click on the **Cog** icon, then select **Schedule report**.

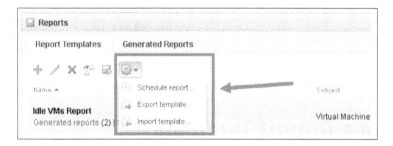

2. In the wizard, navigate the vSphere Hosts and Clusters tree to the object that you want to schedule the Report Template against. By default, vSphere World will be selected. Click on **Next**.

3. In the **Define Schedule** panel, set when you would like the Report Template to be scheduled, and how often.

4. You can optionally define a mail server and/or network share to email or place the scheduled report in.

   An alternate place to define your mail server or network share would be **Administration | Outbound Settings**.

5. Click on **Finish** to complete the creation of the scheduled report.

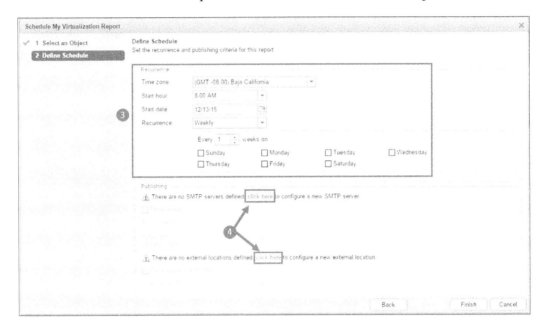

Building a Report Template

Earlier in this chapter, we built some Views. Let's see how we can incorporate those views into a Report Template:

1. Reports are part of Content, so navigate to **Content | Reports**.

2. Click on the *plus* icon to add a new **Report Template**.

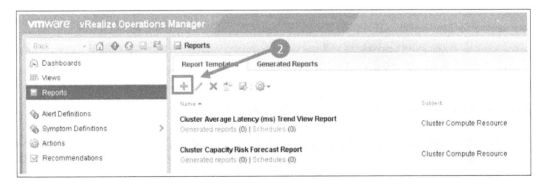

3. Similar to the Views workspace, the **New Template** workspace has a set of steps to follow. The first is to give your Report Template a **Name** and **Description**.

4. Click on **2. Views and Dashboards**.

5. We now need to add the **Views** that we want in the workspace. There are generally a lot of Views to select from, so you will probably need to use the filter box to enter a text filter that will narrow down the search. In the following example screenshot, you can see that I have filtered using the text **My**.

 You will see **Plus** and **Pencil** icons in **2. Views**. You can use these to create and edit Views here, although I would recommend you do it in **Content | Views**.

6. Now, simply drag each View into the middle column in the order you want them to appear in your final Report.

7. If you are building a large report, you can use the **arrows** to collapse or expand the View visualization. The **X** icon is used to delete a View from a Report Template.

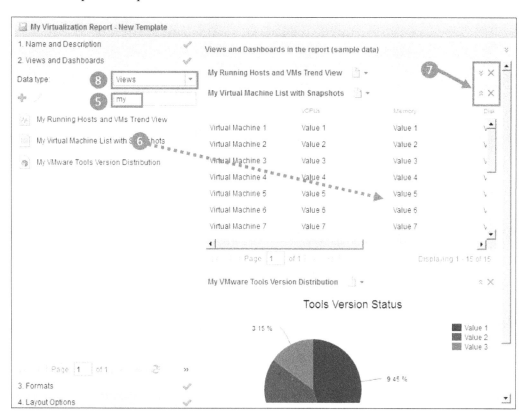

8. Notice the **Data type** dropdown; this allows you to add a Dashboard into your report.

9. Now, click on **3. Formats** to decide what formats you would like the report to be exportable as. You will see you have the option of **.PDF** and **.CSV**. Use the checkboxes to select your required formats.

10. Click on **4. Layout Options** to complete the Report Template. Here, you have three additional items you can add to your report:

    ○ **Cover Page**: When the Report Template is run, a cover page will be created with details about when it was run, who ran the report, and the object on which the report has been run.

      You can optionally add your own image to the cover page, for example, your company or departmental logo, by clicking on **Browse**, and uploading the image.

    ○ **Table of Contents**: This will add a page to the report that lists the Views you have used in the report, and the pages in the report in which they can be found.

    ○ **Footer**: This adds page numbers and the date to the foot of the Report pages.

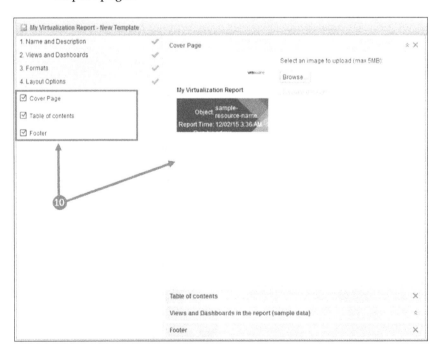

11. Finally, click on **Save** to save the Report Template.

As you will have seen, hopefully, the creation of Views and Reports is a relatively straightforward task, but can lead to some very powerful and visually appealing outcomes.

Managing reports

Similar to Views, as you build the set of Report Templates you are going to use in your environment, you will find the options to manage them very useful. There are three main ways, in which you manage your Report Templates, and they can be found by navigating to **Content | Reports**.

- **Create** or **Delete** Report Templates: Use the green **plus**, or the red **cross** icons to create or delete Report Templates.

- **Clone**: Use the *clone* icon to make a copy of a Report Template.

- **Export** or **Import** Report Templates: Click on the *cog* icon to export or import your Report Templates as XML files. This allows you to copy Report Templates between vRealize Operations instances.

The Reports that you generate can all be found by selecting the **Generated Reports** tab. They will stay in that repository until they are deleted.

To delete Reports that you have generated but no longer need, hold the *Ctrl* and *Shift* keys to multiselect the reports you want to delete, and click on the red X, to delete them.

Summary

In this chapter, we looked at Views and Reports in depth. We started with understanding what Views are, and how to construct them. We built example List, Trend, and Distribution Views. We then looked at how you manage your Views, and use them in Dashboards.

Next we looked at the reporting capability of vRealize Operations. We looked at how you can generate, and schedule generation of Reports using the built-in Report Templates. We then examined how you can take the Views you created to build your own Report Templates.

In the next chapter, we are going to look at how Symptoms, Recommendations, and Actions are the building blocks of the Alerting capabilities in vRealize Operations.

5

Alerts, Symptoms, Recommendations, and Actions

In this chapter, we look into the rich alerting framework that has been introduced into vRealize Operations.

We will start by looking at the structure of alerts, and how a combination of Symptoms, Recommendations, and Actions provide meaningful alerting for the administrator.

Next, we will look at how you can build your own alerts, and apply them to your infrastructure.

Finally, we will look at how you can view and manage your alerts.

Alerts overview

One of the most powerful new features in vRealize Operations is the *Alerting Framework*. The flexibility it provides allows you to use it in a wide variety of ways. Some of the more common use cases are:

- Alerting about performance issues, such as a virtual machine with high *CPU Ready*.

- Assessing and reporting about system configuration. The example we will look at later in this chapter ensures that all your hosts have NTP configured correctly.

- Performing **actions** on objects based on observed symptoms. For example, a virtual machine might experience consistently high CPU utilization, so you might want to add a further vCPU automatically.

Alerts and content

Within vRealize Operations, content is where the capabilities of the vRealize Operations Solutions or Management Packs are defined.

When you install a Solution, or Management Pack, the installation will typically install additional content, such as *Alerts*, *Symptoms*, *Recommendations*, and *Actions*, relevant to the Solution's adapters.

The vSphere Solution is installed automatically, when you install vRealize Operations for the first time.

As you can see in the following screenshot, navigating to **Content | Alert Definitions** will show you some of the alerts that have been defined by the vCenter Adapter:

Similarly, if you look at **Symptom Definitions**, **Actions**, and **Recommendations** in content, you will see which of those have been defined by the vCenter Adapter.

Alert Definitions

An **Alert Definition** is a relatively straightforward construct made up of a number of parts:

- **Symptoms**: These are the conditions under which an alert will be triggered. An alert can have a single symptom or can have multiple symptoms with Boolean logic applied to determine the trigger conditions.

- **Recommendations**: Once an alert is triggered, a list of Recommendations can be provided. These are an ordered set of solutions to resolve the alert condition.

- **Actions**: Recommendations can optionally have Actions associated with them. When they are associated, these Actions carry out the Recommendation.

An example of this is an alert related to *virtual machine high CPU utilization*:

- **Symptom**: The alert will be triggered when one or more metrics related to high CPU is observed

- **Recommendation**: There might be a recommendation to add vCPU to the virtual machine.

- **Action**: Adding vCPU is a predefined action that will be included in the Recommendation.

Let's now look at Symptoms, Recommendations, and Actions in more detail.

Symptom Definitions

As mentioned earlier, it is one or more Symptom Definitions that defines when an alert is triggered. There are four different Symptom Definition types:

- Metric/Property
- Message Event
- Fault
- Metric Event

If you are creating your own custom alerts, you will generally be working with Metric/Property Symptom Definitions. The other three are generally used by vRealize Operations itself, or by Solutions.

Symptom Criticality

The description of every symptom includes its **Criticality**. This is a measure of how important the symptom is. There are four levels of Criticality:

- **Info**: Typically used to describe the object state, for example, **Virtual machine is powered off**, which is a symptom that might be used to suppress alerts that aren't relevant when a machine is powered off

- **Warning**: This is the first level of criticality; this will typically set a badge color yellow

- **Immediate**: This is something that requires immediate attention and the badge color will turn orange

- **Critical**: This is something that is likely to be service impacting—the badge color will be set to red

Metric/Property Symptom Definitions

The first main Symptom Definition type, and the one most commonly used, is the Metric/Property symptom. These are symptoms that are defined by a Metric or Property, having a specific value or having breached a value level.

To look at the list of Metric/Property Symptom Definitions, navigate to **Content | Symptom Definitions**. Let's start by looking at a symptom related to the *CPU Ready* metric.

With a list of 350 symptoms, you will definitely be using the filter options to find the symptoms you are looking for. To search for the '*Virtual machine high ready time on each vCPU*' symptom, simply type 'ready' into the filter box.

You will see that the Metric/Property Symptom Definitions are constructed of eight parts:

- **Name**: This is the name of the Symptom Definition. This should be as meaningful and descriptive as possible.

- **Criticality**: In this case, this is set to critical, as shown by the red triangle. If you hover over the red triangle, it will bring up a text box saying **Critical**.

- **Object type**: Every symptom is defined against a specific object type—in this case, high *ready time* is a *virtual machine* metric.

- **Metric Name**: This is the specific metric that the symptom relates to. In this example, it is the *Ready (%)* metric in the *CPU* branch of the metric tree. It is described as **CPU | Ready (%)** in the UI.

- **Operator**: What operator do we want to apply against the metric for this symptom? In this case, we are looking for high ready time, so the operator is: **is greater than**. High *CPU Ready* will be defined as over a particular value. The operators you can use are:
  - **is greater than**
  - **is greater than or equal to**
  - **is less than**
  - **is less than or equal to**
  - **is**
  - **is not**

- **Value**: This is the value for the metric. In this case, the symptom will be triggered when ready time **is greater than 10%**.

> **Ready time** is a metric commonly monitored by vSphere administrators to determine how well a virtual machine is performing. A value of over 10% will be an indicator of noticeably deteriorating performance.

- **Defined by**: This describes whether the symptom is user defined or defined by one of the Solutions. If it is user defined, the value will be **User**, if defined by a Solution, it will be the name of the adapter in that Solution.

Creating a metric symptom

Let's look at how easy it is to create your own symptom content.

We looked at a critical symptom earlier. In this next scenario, we would like to be warned at a lower threshold of CPU Ready, rather than the out-of-the-box symptom. For this scenario, we will consider a CPU Ready value of **5%** to require attention.

The following steps describe how to build a Symptom Definition to support this requirement.

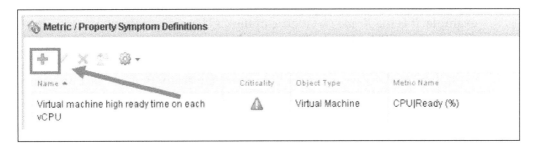

Click on the green *plus* icon to start. First, we need to select our **Base Object Type**:

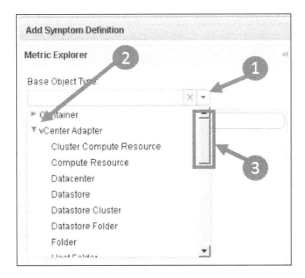

1. Click on the arrow to bring up the selector.
2. Click on the arrow next to vCenter Adapter to expand it. We are looking for the object type **Virtual Machine**, which is defined by the vCenter Adapter.
3. Scroll down to locate the **Virtual Machine** object type and click on it to select. This will open up the metric tree for the virtual machine object type.

4. The preceding critical symptom used the **CPU** | **Ready** (%) metric, so we will use the same one.

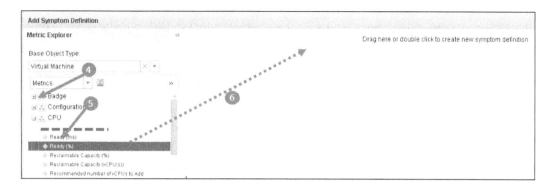

Locate the **CPU** branch of the metric tree and expand it.

5. Scroll down to locate **Ready** (%).

[Note: In the preceding screenshot, the list of metrics has been reduced.]

6. Drag the **Ready** (%) metric into the box in the top box in the right-hand side panel.

Next, we need to configure the settings for this symptom:

7. In the first dropdown, there are two options:

    ◦ **Static Threshold**: This is what we will use; it is a setting defined by the user.

    ◦ **Dynamic Threshold**: Use this if you want to set a symptom based on an object's dynamic threshold. If, for example, you wanted a symptom that triggers when you see unexpected CPU ready. Dynamic Thresholds were covered in *Chapter 1, Introduction to vRealize Operations Manager*.

8. Provide a name for the Symptom Definition. This is how it will appear in the Symptom Definition list. For this Symptom Definition, we will call it **Virtual machine ready time on each vCPU at warning level**.

9. Now we set the criticality. Use the drop-down box to select a **Warning** criticality.

10. Next is the circumstance under which the symptom is triggered. We are going to use **is greater than** and **5,** so that we trigger the symptom when CPU Ready is greater than 5%.

11. Finally, we set the Wait Cycle and Cancel Cycle. First, click on the **Advanced** arrow to open Wait Cycle and Cancel Cycle:

    ◦ **Wait Cycle**: This determines how many times we want to observe the symptom before it is triggered. A wait cycle of 1 would trigger immediately. Setting a number other than 1 would limit the alerting of transient spikes and peaks.

    ◦ **Cancel Cycle**: This determines how many times we want to observe non-symptomatic values, before we cancel the triggered symptom.

> Note the option to **Evaluate on instanced metric**. This would apply the symptom to every vCPU instance instead of the overall vCPU value. In this case, we are interested in ready time across all vCPUs as opposed to each vCPU.

12. Once complete, click on **Save** to save your new Symptom Definition.

You will notice the **Defined by** field in the Symptom Definition list is set to **User** as it is a user-defied symptom.

The new Symptom Definition is now complete and can be consumed by an alert.

Property Symptom Definitions

One of the new key features of vRealize Operations Version 6 was the collection of host system and virtual machine **properties**. These can be used extensively to ensure that the configuration of your environment meets the standards you require.

They are also used to build the **vSphere Hardening Guidelines** compliance alerts, which we will look at later in this chapter.

To get an understanding of how Property Symptom Definitions can be built and used, we will now build one. We will use this later to create an Alert Definition that confirms whether our NTP services are configured correctly.

There are already a number of NTP-based Symptom Definitions available out of the box. You can look at these by navigating to **Content | Symptom Definitions | Metric/Property Symptom Definitions**. As before, use the filter, but this time enter the text **NTP** into the filter box, and hit *Return*:

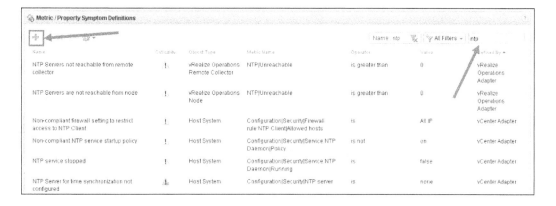

The key property that isn't tested for, however, is the NTP source that is being used. That is because, obviously, everyone uses different NTP sources!

Creating a Property Symptom Definition

It is a straightforward task to setup a Symptom Definition to test for the incorrect NTP server being configured as your source:

 In this particular case, we are going to test for an **incorrect** NTP configuration, as we will use the symptom later to build an alert for incorrect configurations. There might also be cases where you want to test for the **correct** value of a property. It is quite common to see Symptom Definitions for both.

1. First, click on the green *plus* icon to create a new Symptom Definition.

2. Just as when you created the metric symptom previously, navigate to the **vCenter Adapter** inventory tree and select **Host System**.

3. Use the drop down to change the metric tree to the property tree

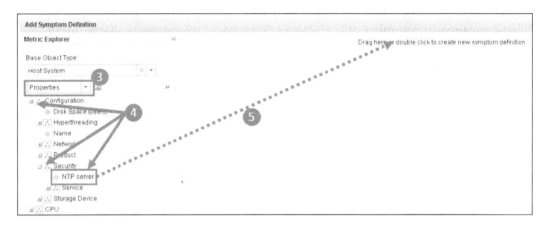

4. This time, expand **Configuration**, then **Security** and locate the **NTP server** property.

5. Drag the NTP Server property to the top box in the right-hand-side panel.

   Now we need to configure the Property symptom:

6. Leave the default of **Static Threshold** in the first box. The alternate of **Compare** would be used if you wanted to compare this property with another property.

7. The symptom needs an appropriate name, **NTP Server is incorrect**.

8. In this case, we are going to set the symptom criticality to **Critical**.

9. Now we set the operand to **Not equal to** and then add the **IP Address** or **FQDN** of our NTP source.

10. Next, click on the arrow to show the **Advanced** settings, and we will set the wait cycle to **1**, and the Cancel Cycle to **1**. A property doesn't tend to be as dynamic as a metric, so if it is incorrect, we just need to know.

11. Finally, click on **Save** to save your new Property Symptom Definition.

We will use this Property Symptom Definition later when we build a new alert.

Message Event Symptom Definitions

Message Event Symptom Definitions are generally defined, either by vRealize Operations itself or by the Solutions you install. They are typically used to provide information about the health of vRealize Operations or the configured adapters.

You can create your own Message Event Symptom Definitions if you have external systems creating events, which you want to react to. You would do this by leveraging the **REST API**, which is now available in vRealize Operations.

Message Event Symptom Definitions can be of the following type:

- **System Performance Degradation**: If you browse the Message Event Symptoms, you will see a lot of vRealize Operations symptoms of this type. These are used to issue alerts about problems with vRealize Operations.

- **Change**: This is used to describe change events. The vCenter Adapter sends change events to vRealize Operations. You might want to, for example, watch for a vMotion event, and correlate it with something else or alert on it.

- **Environment Down**: This is typically used to monitor the health of the vRealize Operations adapters' collections.

- **Notification**: This is for general notifications. For example, there are a number of definitions that describe if your licenses are going to expire or are exceeding limits.

Documentation on using the REST API is available at `http://IPAddressOfNode/suite-api`.

Fault Symptom Definitions

These Symptom Definitions describe faults in your infrastructure that can cause a degradation in service.

They are typically described against events sent from adapters related to faults. For example, if you browse the list of Fault Symptom Definitions, you will see many related to hardware faults detected by system sensors.

Metric Event Symptom Definitions

The final Symptom Definition type is **Metric Event Symptom Definitions**. This Symptom Definition type takes the metric and the threshold from external systems. In practice, it is generally just used by vRealize Operations to act on the hard thresholds defined within itself.

It can also be used by external systems through the REST API.

Recommendations

As mentioned at the beginning of the chapter, alerts are comprised of Symptoms, Recommendations, and Actions. Recommendations are a list of recommendations, of things you should carry out when an alert is triggered.

For example, if a virtual machine experiences high read or write latency, there are a number of things you can do to resolve the problem:

- Use **Storage I/O Controls** (**SIOC**) to govern I/O to the data store
- Add more IOPS to the underlying physical storage
- Perform a vSphere Storage vMotion to move the virtual machine's VMDK to a data store with more I/O capacity

What I have just listed are recommendations, and this is exactly what is meant by vRealize Operations Recommendations.

If you navigate to **Content | Recommendations**, you will see the list of Recommendations available out of the box:

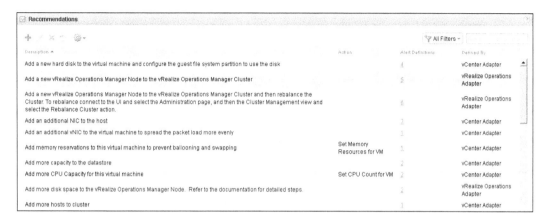

The recommendation itself can be as simple as **Add more hosts to cluster**. Alternatively, it could be an extremely detailed and verbose description of a series of actions you need to carry out to resolve a condition.

Recommendations can also include embedded hyperlinks to web pages, such as VMware KB articles, or, if you create your own recommendation, links to your operational processes or manuals.

In the preceding example, you will see that some Recommendations have **Actions** associated with them. For example, the **Add more CPU Capacity for this virtual machine** Recommendation has the **Set CPU Count for VM** Action associated with it. Actions can carry out the Recommendation described. We will cover Actions in the next section.

Finally, in the Recommendations panel, it is possible to see how many alerts each Recommendation is part of. If you click on the number, a dialogue box will list those alerts.

Creating a Recommendation

Now, we will see how you can create your own Recommendations:

1. Click on the green *plus* icon to open the **New Recommendation** dialogue box:

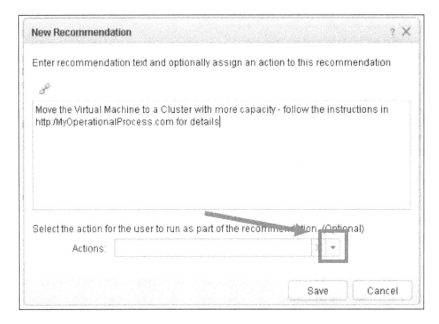

2. Add some free form text to describe the Recommendation.
3. You can optionally select one of the Actions to associate with your Recommendation.
4. Click on **Save**.

It really is as easy as that! Recommendations are a great way of enriching your alerts.

Actions

Recommendations are a list of recommended steps to be taken to resolve a problem or alert. The Actions capability within vRealize Operations allows the vSphere administrator to act on the Recommendation. For example, for the Recommendation **Add CPU Capacity to a Virtual Machine**, an Action that carries out this Recommendation is associated with it.

Out-of-the-box actions are carried out using the vCenter Python Actions Adapter. This runs Python scripts against your vCenter(s) to carry out the tasks defined by the Actions.

Navigate to **Content** | **Actions** to see the list of Actions that are available:

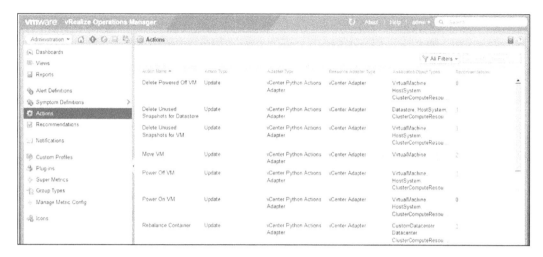

You will see that there are 16 actions and they are all associated with a variety of object types.

Alerts

The alerting framework in vRealize Operations is a very powerful feature of the solution. The ability of Symptoms, Recommendations, and Actions to come together to create meaningful and actionable alerts is something that was missing from previous versions.

As with Symptoms, Recommendations, and Actions, there are a lot of preconfigured Alert Definitions in Content, which are provided by the Solutions you install and configure.

If you navigate to **Content** | **Alert Definitions** you can see a list of all the Alert Definitions available.

Now, let's look at how Alert Definitions are constructed. The best way of doing this is to look at one of the more interesting out-of-the-box alerts:

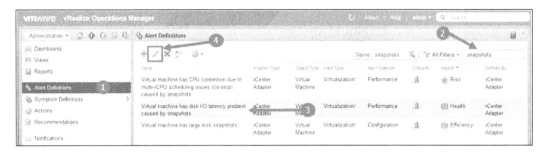

1. Navigate to **Content | Alert Definitions**.

2. We will look at the alerts relating to snapshots, so, type the text `snapshots` into the filter box, and hit **Return** to filter the list.

3. You will see there are three Alert Definitions related to snapshots. Click on **Virtual machine has disk I/O latency problems caused by snapshots** to select it.

4. Click on the pencil icon to edit it. We won't be editing it, but this allows us to look at how it is constructed.

    The Alert Definition Workspace has five elements:

    *   Name And Description
    *   Base Object Type
    *   Alert Impact
    *   Symptom Definitions
    *   Recommendations

    Name and **Description** are self-explanatory. When you build your own Alert Definition, it is well worth using the description box to document your alert. Use it to describe the conditions you are seeking to alert, and the objects you expect to apply the Alert Definition to.

It is also worthwhile setting a standard for the naming of alert. Perhaps, preface them with your company or departmental name.

5. Click on **2. Base Object Type**. This defines the object type that this Alert Definition is going to be associated with. In this case, it is for **Virtual Machines**.

6. Click on **3. Alert Impact**. This defines how the alert is triggered and displayed. It is made of five elements:

  ° **Impact**: This determines which main badge: **Health**, **Risk**, or **Efficiency**, will be affected when the alert is triggered.

  ° **Criticality**: This is the level of criticality for the alert. It can be set to any of the regular criticality levels of Info, Warning, Immediate, or Critical. More commonly, however, is for it to be set to **Symptom Based**. This means the criticality level of the **symptom** is used. If there are multiple symptoms in the Alert Definition, then the highest criticality level of the *triggered* symptoms will be used.

  ° **Alert Type and Subtype**: This classifies the alert, and helps you route it to the most appropriate personnel. It will also define how some of the sub-badges will react. For example, if you set an Alert Definition to be **Virtualization/Hypervisor : Compliance**, it will affect the compliance badge. That alert would also drive the compliance dashboard to display symptoms that are noncompliant.

  ° **Wait Cycle**: The wait cycle determines how many times the triggered symptoms have to be seen before the alert is triggered. For some symptoms, you will want to trigger the alert immediately; others, you might want to wait to see several instances of a condition.

  ° **Cancel Cycle**: The alert will be cancelled based on how many times the symptoms are no longer observed as triggered.

It's important to note that both Wait Cycle and Cancel Cycle are added to the symptom's cycle times. In practice, most Alert Definitions have cycle times of 1 so that they are triggered or cancelled as soon as the associated symptoms are.

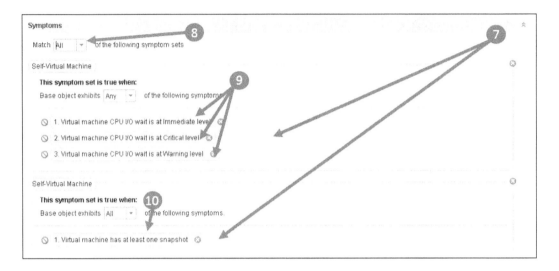

7. Now we should look at the symptoms that are going to cause this alert to trigger. You will see that there are four symptoms in total.

8. There are often some **boolean** conditions in place to determine the triggering of the alert. In this case, we have two **Symptom Sets**, and the logic is set such that the alert will trigger when **All** the sets are matched. Alternatively, this could be set to **Any** of the sets, and the alert will trigger when just one of the sets is matched.

9. In the first Symptom Set, there are three symptoms relating to the level of virtual machine CPU I/O wait. There is a further Boolean condition for these symptoms. In this case, the Symptom Set is true when the base object exhibits **Any** of the symptoms.

   This could also have been set to **All**.

   So, in summary, this Symptom Set has been constructed to watch for rising levels of *CPU I/O wait*. There are symptoms defined for Immediate, Warning, and Critical levels, and the symptom that is triggered will determine the criticality of the alert.

10. The second Symptom Set has just one symptom, which will be triggered when a virtual machine contains one or more snapshots.

So, looking at all the symptoms together, the alert will be triggered, when significant levels of *CPU I/O wait* are observed on VMs, which additionally have a snapshot on them. The criticality of the alert will be set by the criticality of the *CPU I/O wait*.

11. Finally, scroll down to the **Recommendations** panel. Here, you will see the two Recommendations that have been assigned to this Alert Definition:

    ○ **If the virtual machine has multiple snapshots, delete the older snapshot**: This Recommendation is of the highest priority, so it should be the first to be considered. You will see, it also has the action to **Delete Unused Snapshots for VM** associated with it.

    ○ **Reduce the number of snapshots by consolidating the snapshots into 1 snapshot**, with some instructions on how to do this. This is the second Recommendation to be considered.

12. Click on **Cancel** to exit this alert without saving.

As you have seen, the construction of alert Definitions is a relatively straightforward task. You can build very rich Alerts out of the Symptoms, Recommendations, and Actions available to you or the ones that you build yourself.

The alert that we looked at previously is a fairly standard **health** alert—something used to alert on and troubleshoot a performance impacting condition. There are many of these available to you as standard, although you may find that you add to them or modify them to meet your operational imperatives.

vSphere Hardening Guidelines alerts

In *Chapter 2, Install, Configure, and Administer vRealize Operations Manager,* we talked about the initial installation of vRealize Operations. One of the changes we looked at for the Default Policy was to enable the vSphere Hardening Guidelines alerts and apply it to a group of objects.

It's very unlikely your Hosts and VMs will adhere to all the vSphere hardening guidelines. On the other hand, it is very likely that there are a number of hardening guidelines you do wish your vSphere estate to adhere to. In this section, we will look at how you can take advantage of Alert Definitions to modify the guidelines to meet your security requirements.

First, take a look at a typical host in your environment and check its compliance posture with respect to the out-of-the-box hardening guidelines:

 The easiest way to navigate to the Object Dashboard of an object in vRealize Operations is to type part, or all, of its name in the search box in the top-right corner of the UI.

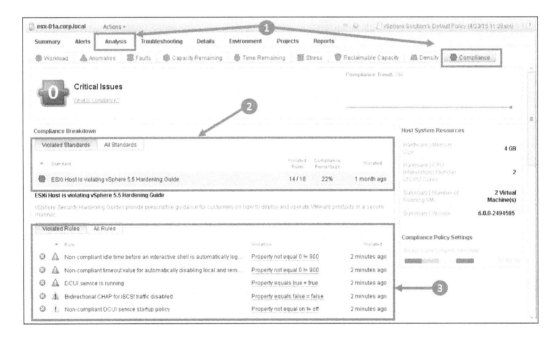

1. In *Chapter 2, Install, Configure, and Administer vRealize Operations Manager*, we created a new policy that added the Hardening Guidelines alerts and we associated the policy with a Custom Group. Navigate to the dashboard of one of your hosts in that Custom Group and click on **Analysis** and then **Compliance** to show the Compliance panel.

2. Notice the **Compliance Standard** that is being violated – the vSphere Hardening Guidelines.

3. Notice all the **Rules** that are causing this standard to be violated. You will probably recognize them as configuration settings that determine how security hardened a host is.

   Obviously, in your environment, it is probable that your host is hardened to your requirements, but, it is worth at this point looking at how that compares with the vSphere Hardening Guidelines to see if there are areas you could, or should, improve on.

   I often find clients have accidently left things such as SSH and DCUI enabled after they have undertaken some troubleshooting. They fix the problem then forget to reharden the hosts.

> You will find the full hardening guidelines whitepapers for all versions of vSphere on VMware's website at `http://www.vmware.com/uk/security/hardening-guides`. These will give you all the information you need in order to fully assess which settings are important in your environment.

   Take a note of the rules that aren't applicable to your environment. In the next step, we are going to remove the unneeded rules, to ensure the guidelines more accurately reflect your requirements.

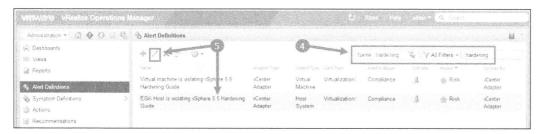

4. Navigate back to **Content** | **Alert Definitions** and filter the list with the text `hardening`.

5. Click on the **ESXi Host is violating vSphere 5.5 Hardening Guide** alert, and then on the **Clone** icon to make a copy.

> When changing out-of-the-box content, it is best practice to first make a copy of the original, and only then, make changes to the cloned content. You can then disable the original content in your policy.

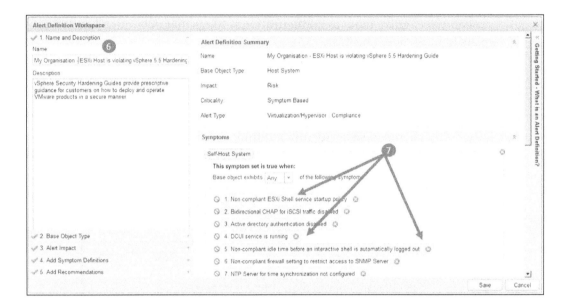

6. Give your hardening guideline a new name, perhaps prefacing with your organization or department's name.

7. You will see that these guidelines are a list of property-based symptoms. Click on the **X** icon on the symptoms you have decided you don't want to be considered when assessing the security settings of your vSphere hosts.

8. Once you have removed the symptoms you want to, click on **Save** to save the new **Alert Definition**.

9. Next, we need to change the **Default Policy** to reflect your organization's security guidelines instead of the standard hardening guidelines.

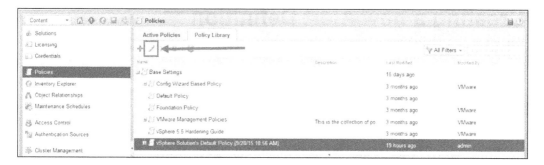

10. Navigate to **Administration | Policies | Policy Library** and expand **Base Settings** to locate your Default Policy. Click on the pencil icon to edit it.

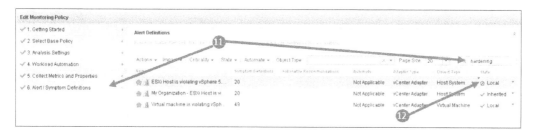

11. Click on the plus sign for **6. Alert/Symptom Definitions**, to expand the section. Add the text `hardening` into the filter field, and hit return to find the relevant alerts.

12. For the original **ESXi Host** is violating guidelines alert, change **State** to **Local** with the red disabled icon. You will notice your new policy is automatically enabled through inheritance, as it becomes part of the default policy.

13. Finally, click on **Save** to save the Policy.

   If you return to your host's object dashboard and look at the **Analysis | Compliance** tab again, you should see your new compliance standard in effect.

 It take a few minutes for the **Compliance** tab to be updated. It is usually done when the vCenter Adapter makes a data collection, which, by default, is every 5 minutes.

Creating a new Alert Definition

Earlier in this chapter, we created a Symptom Definition to test for the correct NTP server being configured. Now that we also know how compliance alerts work, let's create an alert Definition to trigger an Alert when any of the following occur:

- The wrong NTP server is configured
- The NTP service is stopped
- The NTP service is not set to start automatically

With this NTP Alert Definition in place, we will ensure the NTP configuration of our Hosts is always set correctly.

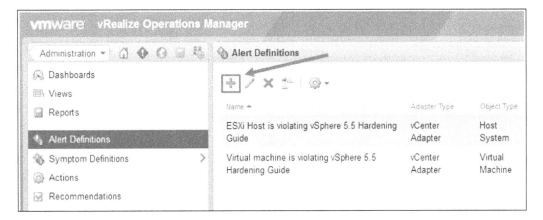

1. Navigate to **Content | Alert Definition** and click on the green **plus** icon to create a new Alert Definition.
2. Give your **Alert Definition** an appropriate name, such as **My NTP Service standard**, and if you wish, a description that explains that it is to check the configuration of your host's NTP service.

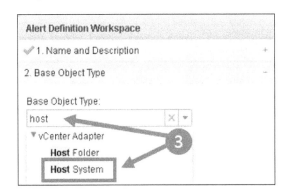

3. Click on **2. Base Object Type**. Type **host** in the field, and then select **Host System**, when the list of Object Types matching **host** appears.

4. Now, click on **3. Alert Impact**, and configure it as follows:

   ° **Impact**: Set this to **Risk**, as these type of compliance alerts are associated with Risk

   ° **Criticality: Symptom Based**

   ° **Alert Type and Subtype**: **Virtualization/Hypervisor : Compliance**

   ° **Wait Cycle**: Set this to **1**, as we want to know immediately

   ° **Cancel Cycle**: Set this to **1**, as we want to cancel immediately

5. Now, we need to add the three symptoms for this Alert Definition. Click on **4. Add Symptom Definitions**.

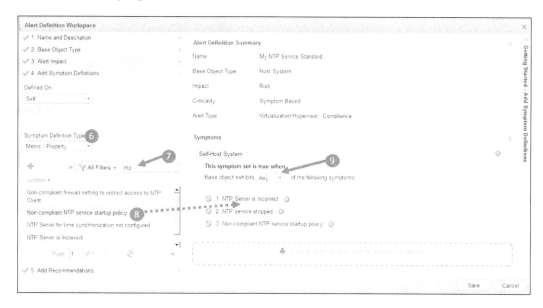

6. The symptoms we are looking for are Property Symptoms, so we can use the default type of **Metric/Property**.

7. Filter for NTP based symptoms by typing `ntp` in the filter box and hitting **Return**.

8. Now, we just need to locate and drag the following symptoms into the panel:

   ° **NTP Server is Incorrect** (this is the custom symptom we created earlier in this chapter)

   ° **NTP Service is stopped**

    ° **Non-compliant NTP service start policy**

[Note: Make sure you drag them into the same Symptom Set as in the preceding screenshot. Do not drag the second and third symptoms into a new Symptom Set.]

9. Change the dropdown to **All**, from **Any**, in the **Base object exhibits...** field.

10. Click on **5. Add Recommendations**.

11. Create a new Recommendation for this Alert Definition. Click on the green **Plus** icon to create one. Add some text into the dialogue box to represent the Recommendation, for example, **Reconfigure this host with the correct NTP service settings as defined in my organization's operational manual**. Click on **Save**, as there are no actions to be associated with this Recommendation.

12. You will need to filter the Recommendations list to find your new Recommendation in the list. Just use the text ntp. Locate your new Recommendation and drag it into the Recommendations field.

13. Finally, click on **Save** to save your new Alert Definition.

As you have seen, creating and constructing Alerts, Symptoms, and Recommendations is a very straightforward task. As you start using them, you will think of more and more ways they can be used to ensure that your operations are running smoothly.

Viewing and managing Alerts

The alerts that are triggered can be viewed and acted on in a number of places. The main places in which you can view, manage, and link to alerts are:

*   The **Recommendations Dashboard**, where all the active alerts for the entire environment being monitored will be displayed in ranked order of importance.

*   The Alerts list: This is where all the alerts are listed and can be filtered and managed.

*   The **Summary** tab of an Object's dashboard: This is where you can see all the alerts for that object and its descendants.

*   The **Alerts** tab of an Object's dashboard: This is the same as the Alerts list, but is filtered to alerts relevant only to that Object.

- The **Troubleshooting** tab of an Object's dashboard: Here, the alerts can be presented on the Timeline and Events panels. This allows you to visualize alerts in conjunction with and in the context of other Events and Metrics and also other Objects.

Alerts can also be displayed as content in Views, Reports, and Custom Dashboards.

When selecting objects in various parts of the UI, there will also often be a red triangle Alerts icon, which, when clicked on, will bring up a dialogue box with a clickable list of alerts for that object.

Finally, alerts can also be sent to administrators and operators using the notifications capability.

Viewing Alerts

The first place most people will see an alert is in the Recommendations dashboard:

The preceding screenshot shows the alerts currently active in my environment, and includes the NTP alert we created earlier. You will notice, it also shows the number of objects impacted, and the Recommendation we created earlier.

If we click on the **My NTP Services standard** alert, it will bring up a list of the objects with that alert currently active. We can then select the alert for a specific object, and look at the Alert Detail:

The preceding Alert Detail screen shows all the information pertinent to the alert:

- **Criticality**: Represented by the red Risk badge, we can see this is a critical alert.

- **Recommendations**: We see the Recommendations associated with the alert.

- **What is causing the issue?**: The triggered symptoms and their detail. The above is a property symptom, so it shows the history of the property value. For a metric symptom, we would also see a sparkline of that metric.

- **Non-triggered Symptoms** and their values.

- **Alert Information**: This is the detail on the alert itself.

At the top, we have five action icons. These allow the administrator to:

- **Cancel the Alert**: This turns the alert inactive, so it will no longer be displayed or impact badge colors. If the underlying problem is not resolved, however, it will trigger again!

- **Suspend the Alert**: This allows you to suspend the alert for a number of minutes. You will use this if you are working on the alert, or if it was a known problem that is going to go away.

- **Take Ownership**: If you are working on the alert, you can let others know by taking ownership. This means people know the alert is being acted on.

- **Release Ownership**: When you are no longer working on an alert, you can release ownership.

- **Go to Alert Definition**: This will navigate you to the Alert Definition in Content.

Finally, at the top of the screen are some Troubleshooting tabs for the Object that triggered the alert.

Managing Alerts

The main place for managing alerts is the **Alert List**. You navigate here from **Home** by clicking on **Alerts**:

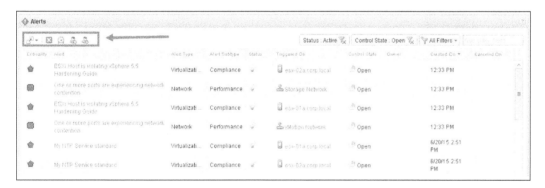

The Alert List shows all the key information about all the alerts within vRealize Operations. The key features of this dashboard are:

- The columns are all sortable by clicking on the column heading.

- You can **Filter** extensively to search for specific information. In the preceding example, I have filtered for **Active** alerts that are currently **Open**.

- Each alert is clickable to take you to the Alert Details screen or to the Object that the alert is triggered on.

- Apart from the four action icons you see in the Alert Details screen, which we described earlier, there is an additional one: **Open in External Application**. When you select an alert, this icon gets activated, and will give you a dropdown to launch an external application in the context of the object the alert relates to.

  For example, if you selected an alert for a Host System, you would have the option of launching the **vSphere Web Client** or **Log Insight** in the context of that Host System. We will look at Log Insight and its integration with vRealize Operations in *Chapter 9, vRealize Log Insight Integration*.

Summary

In this chapter, we looked at the alerting capability of vRealize Operations.

We examined how Alert Definitions are constructed out of Symptoms, Recommendations, and Actions, and we used the framework to build our own custom content, to help monitor and manage the NTP services on our hosts.

Finally we looked at how alerts can be viewed and managed.

In the next chapter, we are going to look at the capacity planning functionality within vRealize Operations.

6
Capacity Planning and Capacity Projects

In this chapter, we are going to explore the capacity planning capabilities of vRealize Operations. The topics that we will look at are as follows:

- Which Capacity model to deploy – allocation or demand?
- Capacity dashboards and badges in vRealize Operations
- Forward planning with capacity projects

Capacity planning for virtual infrastructure

Before we start looking at the capacity planning features in the vRealize Operations solution, it is worth taking a step back to understand how you want to account for capacity in your environment.

This is fundamental to ensuring that vRealize Operations delivers on your organization's capacity planning operational imperatives. I spend a lot of time with vSphere administrators talking through this, as it can have a profound effect on how capacity is reported in vRealize Operations.

Principles of Demand and Allocation capacity planning models

The key to effective capacity planning, in a virtual infrastructure, is deciding where and when you want to use a **Demand**-based model, and where you want to use a model based on **Allocation**.

To understand this better, let's consider a typical virtual machine with the following resources:

- 2x vCPUs
- 4GB RAM
- 40GB disk

How much capacity is this virtual machine consuming?

The answer to this question can vary enormously, depending on who you ask, the importance of the virtual machine, and the amount of resources being demanded.

The two models of Demand and Allocation would describe this virtual machine's capacity consumption as follows:

- **Demand model**: With this model, we would only count capacity as consumed if it is actually being used by the virtual machine. So, in the preceding example, if only CPU cycles equivalent to 1 vCPU, 1 GB RAM, and 10 GB disk were being used, then that is how much capacity that object needs.
- **Allocation model**: With the Allocation model, if we have allocated resources to an object, then these resources should be considered consumed.

These models, therefore, can provide very different answers to how much capacity you are consuming, and both can be equally valid.

Imagine that we have an environment with 1,000 virtual machines, with the resources allocated, and with a demand profile, as described earlier. To support this environment, you would need the following resources:

Demand Model	Allocation Model
1,000 physical CPUs	2,000 physical CPUs
1TB physical RAM	4TB physical RAM
10TB storage	40TB storage

How you decide to account for capacity will depend entirely on your attitude towards risk. I usually describe the vSphere administrator's view of the two ends of the spectrum as follows:

- *I prefer the Allocation model*: If I've assigned specific resources to a virtual machine, it may consume all of those resources, so I can't use any of them for other workloads.
- *I prefer the Demand model*: In a vSphere environment, all of my resources are pooled, so I just need a pool of resources to support my combined workload.

The *answer*, in a real world vSphere environment, usually sits somewhere in between. Also, it probably changes depending on whether you are considering production workloads or test/development workloads.

There will also be a dependency on the resource dimension that you are considering.

 I presented this once at the London **VMware User Group** (**VMUG**). Mike Laverick commented that a purely demand-based model is for the gung-ho administrator and the Allocation model is for the ultra-conservative.

Resource dimensions

Every object type within vRealize Operations has a number of resource dimensions that should be considered when measuring capacity. For example, the **Cluster Compute Resource** object type has the following resource dimensions:

- **CPU**
- **Memory**
- **Disk Space**
- **Disk I/O**
- **Network I/O**
- **vSphere Configuration Limits**

The most *constrained* resource dimension determines whether a cluster still has capacity available and determines how much is available for additional workload.

For example, if your cluster is out of capacity because all of its memory is consumed, it doesn't matter how much CPU or disk resource it has left, your cluster is out of capacity and cannot support any more workload.

Overallocation

As described earlier, the Allocation model can be very conservative, particularly for some of the more easily pooled resource dimensions such as CPU.

Because of this, many administrators will use an Allocation model but will also apply an *overallocation ratio* to their physical resources. For example, with CPU, they may decide that a ratio of 4:1 is appropriate — for them, a physical CPU core may be able to support four vCPUs.

I sometimes consider overallocation a relatively poor workaround to an overly conservative allocation capacity model.

If, as an administrator, you have accepted that a vSphere environment can pool and share resources, applying an arbitrary overallocation ratio seems to be less effective than using empirical resource performance and demand metrics.

One of the benefits of vRealize Operations is that you get the visibility into utilization and capacity that you need in order to move to more-efficient capacity models.

Selecting a capacity planning model

Considering the above-mentioned points, the next question that you need to answer is *Which model should I select?*

This is where vRealize Operations excels. Your choice of model can be extremely granular—you can choose different models for each and every object type and for every resource dimension where appropriate.

These are defined in **policies**. This means that different capacity planning policies can be applied to different sets of objects.

For example, a fairly relaxed policy may be set as the default policy. You may then have a more conservative policy defined for some business critical applications, where it is imperative that resources be ring fenced.

There are various different approaches that can be taken, and I tend to make the following recommendations, at least for the initial configuration:

- **CPU**: Use a **Demand** model, particularly if you have technology such as DRS in use. vSphere is very good at pooling CPU resources, and any unused CPU resources from a virtual machine are generally available for consumption by other virtual machines. There are other levers in the policy settings that can ensure you don't encounter contention.

- **Memory**: Start with an **Allocation** model. Although memory is pooled and there are technologies available, such as TPS, Ballooning, and Compression, to support overallocation, the reclamation of these resources is not as effective or instantaneous as it is with CPU. You may also be able to apply an overallocation ratio to this once you have visibility of your workloads.

  We will look at how you can optimize the allocation of memory later in this chapter.

- **Disk**: Use a **Demand**-based model. If you are using vSphere thin provisioning, then only a Demand-based model is appropriate. If you use vSphere thick provisioning, a Demand-based model can additionally highlight the wasted resources for **reclamation**.

- **Disk I/O and Network I/O**: These are optional for the capacity planning consideration, but I generally recommend using them with a **Demand**-based model.

- **vSphere Configuration Limits**: No choice is available as these are fixed.

 When you set a Policy to Allocation, you should actually set it to Allocation and Demand. The Capacity Planning engine will use the more constrained of Allocation and Demand. This will almost always be Allocation; however, it could be Demand, if you have not allocated sufficient resources to a given object. You certainly want your Capacity Planning model to report when Demand has exceeded the resources available!

These guidelines should be a good starting point for you. As you develop your expertise in this area and as vRealize Operations learns more about your environment, you will probably adapt your approach.

The key is to take the information that vRealize Operations is providing you and use it to make informed decisions about your environment.

Crafting your Capacity Planning policies

Now that we have described the differences between Allocation- and Demand-based models, let's take a look at how you can reflect your requirements in your **Default Policy**. There are number of different ways to craft your policies.

A set of out-of-the-box policies is available, which can be used as a starting point, or you can modify the default policy, which was created during installation when the vSphere Solution was installed and configured.

Given that you probably want to fine-tune your policy, modifying your default policy is generally the best way to start.

Modifying your Default Policy

Here are the steps that you can follow to set your Default Policy to meet your Capacity Planning imperatives.

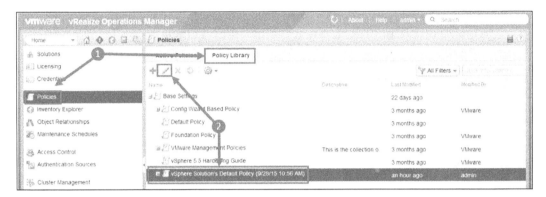

1. Navigate to **Administration | Policies**, and select the **Policy Library** tab.

2. Select **vSphere Solution Default Policy (dated)**, and click on the *Pencil* icon to edit it.

   The Policy section for Capacity Planning is in **3. Analysis Settings**.

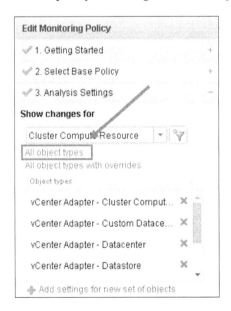

3. We probably want to look at Policy for all our object types, so click on **All object types** to add every object type to the main panel if required.

 By default, the only object types that have had Policy changes made will already be in the main panel. These initial changes will have been made on the basis of the choices you made in the *Define Monitoring Goals wizard* that we looked at in *Chapter 2, Install, Configure, and Administer vRealize Operations Manager*.

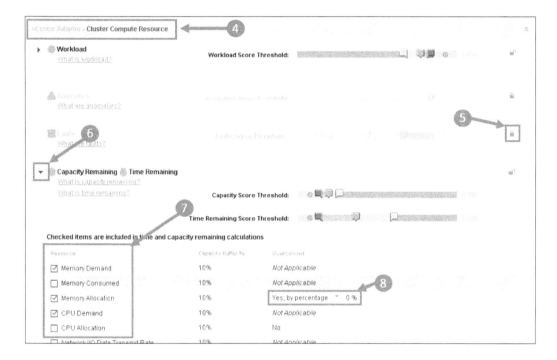

4. We will need to consider changes for every object type—the first one is for **Cluster Compute Resource**.

5. The lock for the first **Policy Element** that we want to make changes to, **Capacity Remaining/Time Remaining**, will be unlocked if changes to base settings have already been made.

   If changes haven't been made and you want to make the changes, then click on the lock to unlock it.

6. If required, click on the *arrow* to expand the section.

7. Now, we need to select the items that we want to include in the time and capacity remaining calculations. This is where you decide the capacity model(s) that you want this policy to adopt. As discussed in the section earlier, I usually start with the following:

   ○ **Memory Demand** and **Memory Allocated** selected. This will set the Policy to have both a Demand and an Allocation model. As you will see later, this will provide a conservative model appropriate for the memory dimension and allow you to visualize the memory demand in the dashboard.

   Notice the **Memory Consumed** option. This reflects the memory consumed metrics you see in vCenter and is an alternative, more conservative, reflection of memory demand.

   ○ **CPU Demand** selected. This will set a CPU Demand model in this policy.

8. You can set an **overcommit** ratio if required. I generally start with no overcommit (0%), but if you do overcommit, you can account for it here.

If you do follow a CPU Allocation model in your organization with a set vCPU to physical CPU ratio that you work to, you can also select the CPU Allocation item and apply your overcommit ratio. Similar to how we will show this with memory later, this will allow you to visualize how that model compares with a CPU demand model.

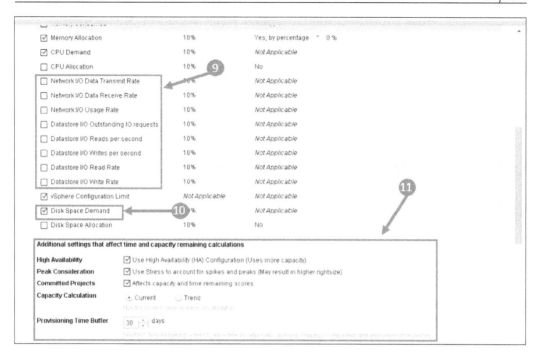

9. Now, scroll down and look at the other items that you can select.

   You can turn on capacity planning for **Network** and **Datastore I/O**. I tend to leave these turned off, at least initially, as it does take time for vRealize Operations to learn how much I/O is available, so it can be difficult to interpret the results. This can detract from the core requirement of analyzing the computing and storage space.

   Once you have got to grips with the solution, however, you should probably turn some of these on.

10. Ensure that **Disk Space Demand** is selected and that **Allocation** is not.

11. The Additional Settings options available are as follows:

    ○ **High Availability (HA)**: Leaving this selected will mean that the capacity calculations will take your HA configuration into account and not use the computing space set aside for HA failover as usable capacity.

- ○ **Peak Consideration**: In general, leave this selected. This means that **Stress** will be considered and effectively means that the high watermark value of demand is the value used for determining an object's demand.

- ○ **Committed Projects**: This determines whether projects defined in Capacity Projects should be used in the capacity calculations. We will look at Capacity Projects later in this chapter.

- ○ **Provisioning Time Buffer**: This determines how much time is removed from time remaining to account for how long it takes you to commission more capacity.

  One example where you may change this is for storage — it may take several months for you to be able to procure more storage, in which case, you can include that lead time in this setting.

12. Now, scroll down and expand each **vCenter Adapter Object Type** in turn by using the arrow shown in the preceding screenshot.

    Make the required changes to **Capacity Remaining/Time Remaining Policy Elements,** as described earlier, for each of the remaining object types.

13. Finally, once complete, click on **Save** to save your updated Default Policy.

When you make changes to the policy elements that effect capacity planning calculations, your dashboards won't reflect all these changes immediately. Most of the capacity planning calculations are performed only once every 24 hours, so it may take that long for your changes to fully come into effect.

Additionally, as most of the results are trend based, **Date Range** in the **Time** policy element will also be considered. Therefore, I always like to make my main changes as soon as I install vRealize Operations. If I make major changes to an instance that has been running for some time, it can take a while for vRealize Operations to age out the historical capacity calculations based on the previous policy. This means it may be up to 30 days before the time remaining badge fully reflects everything.

Finally, if you have just installed vRealize Operations, it will take several days for some of the badges to be calculated as they need several days' worth of data to reflect a trend view.

Now that we know how the Demand and Allocation capacity models work, and we have changed our policy to reflect how we want to account for capacity in our environment, we can look at how vRealize Operations is reporting and managing capacity.

Capacity planning dashboards, views, and reports

The capacity planning capabilities of vRealize Operations are one of the most powerful features of the solution. They will help you to do the following:

- Never run out of capacity
- Always know how much additional workload can be supported
- Know when you are going to run out of capacity and the resource dimension that is most constrained
- Understand where you have the most capacity and where you are the most constrained
- Improve the utilization of the compute and storage investments that you have made
- Optimize your Virtual Machine density
- Identify where you are wasting resources

You will achieve these by using a combination of dashboards, views, and reports.

I always start with the **Capacity Remaining** dashboard.

The Capacity Remaining dashboard

Every object in vRealize Operations can have capacity remaining and a badge score calculated. The Capacity Remaining dashboard displays the details of this analysis.

 Some object types within vRealize Operations do not have a capacity model defined and therefore, do not have a Capacity Remaining dashboard or badge score calculated. For these objects, the dashboard and badge will be grayed out.

You will use the information in the Capacity Remaining dashboard in different ways, depending on the object type that you are looking at.

For high-level objects, such as datacenters and clusters, it's generally to do with *How many more workloads can I run on this object before I have to purchase more hardware?*

For lower-level objects, such as Virtual Machines or datastores, it is more about *Will I need to add resources to support the current and predicted workloads, or can I reclaim some resources for other workloads?*

A **Cluster Compute Resource** object is usually a good place to get an understanding of your capacity utilization. Navigate through **Environment | vSphere Hosts and Clusters**, and select a **Cluster Compute Resource** object in the tree hierarchy.

1. To see the Capacity Remaining dashboard, select **Analysis** and then **Capacity Remaining**.

2. The main graphic to consider in the dashboard is the **Capacity Remaining Breakdown** bar chart.

   In the preceding example, it shows that I have the following:

   ° **Black**: 28% of the total capacity not available as it is needed for **HA** and headroom **Buffers**.

   ° **Green**: Of the remaining **Useable Capacity**, I am using 89%. Note: this is the lighter shaded grey section forming the left part of the bar chart in the preceding image.

   ° **Blue**: I have 11% of the remaining Useable Capacity available for new workloads in this cluster. *Note that my Badge score of 11 reflects this value.* Note: this is the small mid-shaded grey section forming the middle part of the bar chart in the preceding image.

   It's a relatively simple graphic but extremely powerful.

3. The **What Will Fit** section describes the available capacity, in terms of the quantity of virtual machines, of various sizes, that could be supported.

   Large, **Medium**, **Small**, and **Average Profiles** represent the distribution of your Virtual Machine sizes in the object concerned.

   Notice the box with just a *Plus* sign. You may want to know how many Virtual Machines of a particular size will fit in the available capacity remaining. Clicking on this box will allow you to create a **Custom Profile** to define this Virtual Machine size.

4. Now, we can analyze what 11% **Remaining Capacity** means.

As mentioned earlier in this chapter, capacity is measured in a number of resource dimensions. If you scroll down, you will see the calculated resource dimensions for this object.

	Total Capacity	Buffers	Usable Capacity	Value	Recommended Size	Remaining
▶ CPU	456 GHz Configured	HA (21.05%) +10%	324 GHz 71.05% of Total	59.79% 1‍3.71 GHz Demand	76.6 % 248.19 GHz Demand	23.4 % 75.81 GHz
▼ Memory	320 GB Configured (Includes overcommit) Overcommit 1.0:1	HA (20%) +10%	230.4 GB 72% of Total	90.28% 208 GB Allocation	88.51 % 203.92 GB Allocation	11.49 % 26.48 GB
▶ Demand	320 GB Configured	HA (20%) +10%	230.4 GB 72% of Total	40.91% 94.25 GB Demand	51.46 % 118.55 GB Demand	48.54 % 111.85 GB
▶ Allocation	320 GB Configured (Includes overcommit) Overcommit 1.0:1	HA (20%) +10%	230.4 GB 72% of Total	90.28% 208 GB Allocation	88.51 % 203.92 GB Allocation	11.49 % 26.48 GB
▶ Disk Space	1.17 TB Configured	-- +10%	1.05 TB 90% of Total	55.56% 600 GB Demand	55.56 % 600 GB Demand	44.44 % 480 GB
vSphere Configuration	2,560 Virtual Machine(s)		2,560 Virtual Machine(s)	1.64% 42 Virtual	2.11 % 54.14 Virtual	97.89 %

It is the most **constrained** resource dimension that determines the remaining capacity, and in this case, we can see that it is **Memory**, which is the most constrained. This is highlighted by a slight graying of that resource row. The details in the row are also very meaningful:

- ◦ **Total Capacity**: amount of physical RAM available – 320GB

- ◦ **Buffers**: resources that are unavailable for workload, due to **HA** requirements, and a headroom **buffer**. We configured these when we modified the default policy

    In this case, with a 5-node cluster, I have defined one server for HA failover, so vRealize Operations has calculated that 20% is unavailable, leaving 80% useable capacity.

I have also configured a 10% **buffer** of this remaining capacity that I don't want to use: 10% of 80% is an additional 8%. So, the total HA and headroom buffer is 28%.

  ° **Useable Capacity**: Remaining capacity — 72% or 230.4GB.

  ° **Peak Value**: Observed highest value — 90%, or 208GB of the 230.4GB Useable Capacity.

  ° **Recommended Size**: Size that vRealize Operations considers appropriate for this resource dimension. In this case, it is recommended that the clusters have 203 GB to cater for the allocated memory.

  ° **Remaining Value**: Resources remaining for new workloads — 11.5%.

    If you look at the remaining values for all the resource dimensions, you will see that 11.5% is the lowest; therefore, it is this resource, memory, that is the most constrained.

5. Clicking on the arrow next to **Memory** opens up the Demand and Allocation calculations.

    Earlier in this chapter, we configured our capacity policy for memory to be based on **allocated** memory.

    It is useful, however, to understand how much of that allocated memory is actually being **demanded** or used.

    You will see that although we have allocated 88.5% of our resources, if we were to consider a Demand-based capacity model, we would only be consuming 51% of our resources, with 49% available for new workloads.

    This tells me, as a whole, that I have allocated too much RAM to my Virtual Machines. If I were to allocate less, I would yield more resources for more workload.

    Given that memory is my most constrained resource, there is probably some value in doing this.

As you can see, the analysis is very detailed, but extremely clear, and helps you to understand your overall position with respect to capacity, the number of Virtual Machines you can add, and the location of your resource *pinch points*.

Hopefully, this also brings to life the importance of crafting your policies to meet your operational imperatives.

In the Policy section, we talked about a reasonable approach of using an Allocation model for measuring memory capacity.

If you see a large discrepancy between Allocation and Demand, it will help you understand if this is the right way for you to go and, whether to achieve better operational efficiency, you should consider some right sizing or modifying your policy to consider overallocation.

> Every object potentially has this Capacity Remaining dashboard available. To look for outliers, or capacity-constrained resources, use the **Environment** tab (the skittle view) and change the badge to **Capacity Remaining**. You can also use the sort dropdown to group all the constrained objects together.

The Time Remaining dashboard

Along with a Capacity Remaining dashboard, every object also has a **Time Remaining** dashboard.

I sometimes describe this as, arguably, the most important capacity metric of all. If I want to account for the current, predicted, and known workload demand, knowing when I will run out of capacity is key.

If I know that I am not going to run out of capacity any time soon, I can almost forget about day-to-day capacity management until the solution advises me of a change in the situation.

This is exactly what the Time Remaining badge and dashboard do.

The Time Remaining dashboard is quite similar to Capacity Remaining in that it takes into account the most **constrained** resource dimension and is driven by the Policy that you set with respect to Allocation and Demand.

To see the Time Remaining dashboard, select **Analysis** and then **Time Remaining**.

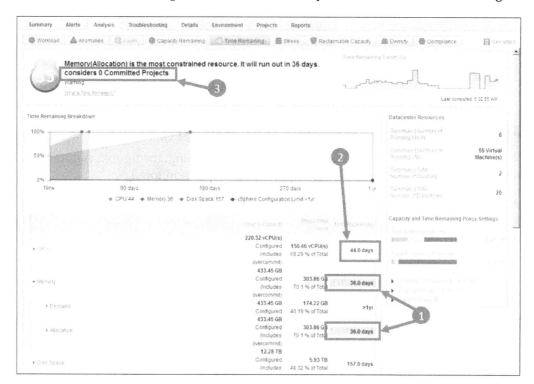

1. In the preceding example, you can see that the most constrained resource is, again, **Memory**, and it is **Allocated Memory**, with only **36.0 days** left before it is consumed.

   This is also called out in the text next to the badge.

2. You can also see that close behind is CPU demand, with only **44.0 days** left. The preceding figure shows this.

   An analysis of this information, therefore, suggests that we probably need to address both memory and CPU constraints.

 There is also a provisioning buffer in effect here. By default, this will be 30 days, allowing extra time to provision for additional resources. In reality, therefore, in the above example, memory and CPU will only actually be consumed in 66 and 74 days, respectively.

3. Finally, notice that the dashboard reflects **0 Committed Projects**. **Capacity Projects** are an additional capability within vRealize Operations through which you can include known future workload or resource additions/ deletions and reflect them in forward-looking analysis, such as Days Remaining.

We will look at Capacity Projects later in this chapter.

Reclaimable Capacity dashboard

When we look at Capacity Remaining and Time Remaining, the figures, naturally, reflect the configuration and sizing of the objects being monitored.

As you seek to **Optimize** your infrastructure, perhaps to remediate a situation where a managed object, such as a cluster, is becoming constrained for resources, it is useful to know how much, and where, there may be resources that can be reclaimed.

This is particularly the case where you are using an Allocation capacity model – if you have allocated resources and they are not being used, then they are effectively consumed and therefore wasted.

Similarly with storage, Virtual Machines will generally consume storage even if they are powered off or idle.

The Reclaimable Capacity dashboard allows you, at a glance, to see where you can reclaim this wasted capacity.

The main areas considered for reclamation are as follows:

- **Oversized Objects**: When an object has too many resources assigned, these additional resources can be considered waste.

You may need to take a pragmatic view on some oversized reporting. For example, a Virtual Machine with four vCPUs, instead of the recommended size of one vCPU, will report wasted vCPU. With vSphere, however, you automatically get much of this unused resource back, so should this really be considered wasted resource?

Of course, as you drive up the CPU utilization of your hosts and clusters, you also need to ensure that you don't drive it too high such that contention occurs and breaches your performance SLA.

Similarly, when using a thin provisioned disk, oversized VMDKs or file systems are mostly irrelevant.

- **Idle Virtual Machines**: Virtual Machines that are idle can be considered reclaimable resources. These have been identified as virtual machines that have been running for some time and may no longer be in use.

- **Powered Off Virtual Machines**: As described earlier, a powered-off Virtual Machine still consumes valuable storage resources.

- **Snapshots**: Along with creating a performance or availability issue, old disk snapshots can consume significant amounts of storage.

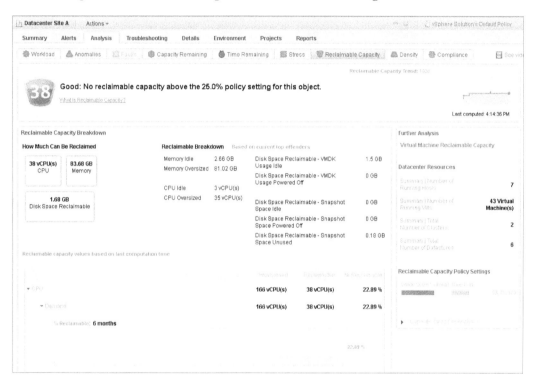

The dashboard itself is fairly self-explanatory, providing a summary of the resources that can be reclaimed, together with details on memory, CPU, disk space, and snapshots.

If the dashboard context is a container object, such as a **Cluster Compute Resource**, you can scroll down to look at the details of the reclaimable capacity of child objects.

Configuring Policy for Reclaimable Capacity

In order for vRealize Operations to accurately identify and report on Reclaimable Capacity, you will almost certainly need to check whether the **Reclaimable Capacity Policy Elements** are correctly set for the **Virtual Machine** object type.

Every object type can have Reclaimable Capacity policy elements. It's unlikely that you will need to make policy changes to object types other than Virtual Machine; however, they can be made if needed. For example, you may want to make a policy change for a cluster compute resource that is reserved for disaster recovery purposes.

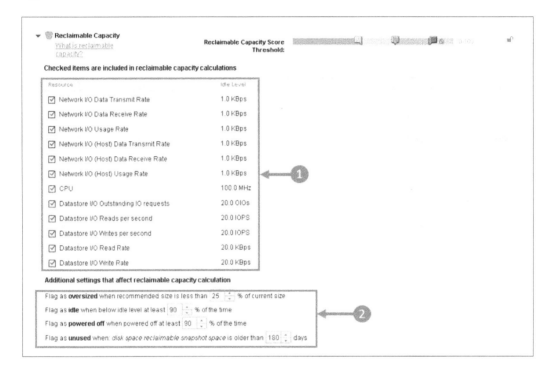

The Reclaimable Capacity policy elements for Virtual Machines can be seen in the preceding screenshot. The changes that you may need to consider are as follows:

1. **Resource Idle levels**: Even if a Virtual Machine is idle, there will still be occasional network and disk I/O, and CPU utilization observed.

   The default values will generally by fine; however, if you have more impactful backup or anti-virus activity, you may need to increase the values.

2. **Additional settings** that add flags to Virtual Machines are as follows:

   ° **Flag as Oversized when**: If the value is set to the default of 25%, this means that objects will not be flagged as **Oversized,** unless they are more than *four times* larger than what vRealize Operations considers an appropriate size.

It is inevitable that all objects will be oversized, even by just a small amount. This flag allows you to report on the objects that are oversized to the largest extent.

It would be quite common to see this increased to 50% so that machines twice as large as their optimal size are flagged.

- ° **Flag as Idle when**: This is used in conjunction with the preceding mentioned Resource Idle Levels. The default of 90% is usually appropriate.

- ° **Flag as Powered off when**: This determines how long a machine should be powered off for in order for it to be considered powered off. A default value of 90% caters to environments where machines may be powered on for operational tasks, such as patching.

  It is quite common to see this default value increased.

- ° **Flag as Unused – Snapshots**: I consider the default value of 180 days to be much too high. When I talk about this value with vSphere administrators, it is extremely common for them to want to see this at 7 days or fewer.

Summary metrics

As well as determining how vRealize displays and visualizes capacity data, the abovementioned Policy settings set the status of some summary metrics ,or flags, as they are described earlier.

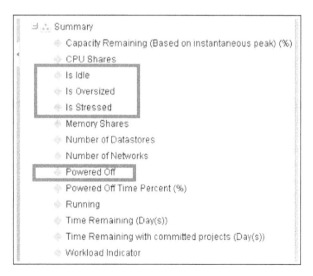

If you browse the metric tree for a Virtual Machine object, you can see some of the following metrics:

- **Is Idle**
- **Is Oversized**
- **Is Stressed**
- **Powered off**

The metrics are set to 0 or 1 depending on the calculated state of the object. These metrics are used quite extensively as filters for views and reports, as we will see later.

 The summary metrics for all objects can be very useful in areas other than Capacity reporting for creating or filtering views and reports.

Capacity Views and Reports

The Capacity dashboards provided by vRealize Operations are very rich; however, sometimes, you may want to look at how capacity is being consumed in your infrastructure in different ways.

In the previous chapter, we examined how Views and Reports are built up — these constructs have been used quite extensively to build Content relevant to capacity planning that you can use out of the box.

It is worth spending some time looking through the available Views to find those that may be relevant to or useful for your organization.

 Generally speaking, the out-of-the-box views have a report template associated with them on a one-to-one basis. For example, the **Idle Virtual Machines View** is the view that is used in the **Idle VMs Report** report template. In this section, we will only look at views and not report templates — you will find that there will always be an associated report template that you can use to export View data.

Virtual Machine views

Capacity-focused views for Virtual Machines are generally **List** or **Distribution** views. You will run these against higher-level objects such as Cluster Compute Resource or Datacenter in order to get a list of Virtual Machines with certain characteristics.

If you navigate to **Content | Views** and then add a filter changing the **subject** to **Virtual Machine**, you can browse all the Virtual Machine views. Some of the views that you will find most useful are as follows:

- **Idle Virtual Machines**: A list of all Virtual Machines with the **Is Idle** metric set. The list shows the metrics that define the Virtual Machines' idle state, and the memory and disk resources that they consume.

- **Powered off VMs**: A list of all Virtual Machines with the **Powered Off** metric set. This list shows the CPU and memory resources that these Virtual Machines are consuming.

- **Virtual Machine Reclaimable Capacity**: List of all Virtual Machines, displaying the reclaimable CPU, memory, and disk space that has been calculated for each.

- **Virtual Machine Recommended CPU and Memory Size**: A list of **Stressed** Virtual Machines, using the **Summary | Is Stressed** metric as a filter. The view shows the current and recommended CPU and memory configurations.

- **Virtual Machine Rightsizing CPU, Memory and Disk Space**: A list of Virtual Machines, filtered with the **Oversized** and **Powered on** metrics, showing details of the current and recommended CPU, memory, and disk space.

 The views mentioned in the preceding section use the flags that we looked at earlier in this chapter in the *Reclaimable Capacity dashboard* section.

As you can see, the list is quite varied and some of the views are very specific, perhaps focusing on just Stressed Virtual Machines.

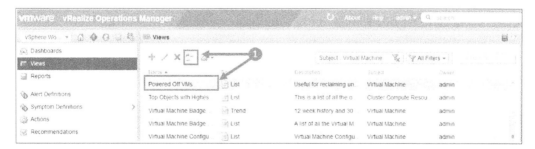

You will often want to change the view to meet your requirements or to add more data. For example, the **Powered off VMs** view would benefit with the addition of details on reclaimable disk. Here is an example of how you would do this:

1. Select the **Powered off VMs** view, and click on the *Clone* icon to clone it.

 You should always **clone** out-of-the-box content as opposed to editing it. This means that future content updates will not overwrite your changes.

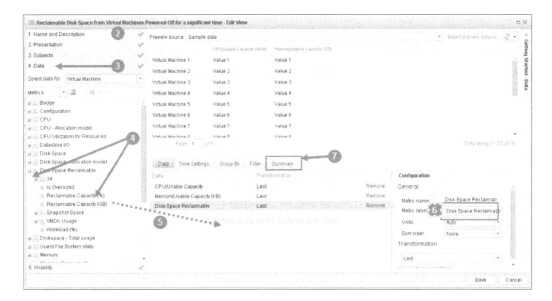

2. Change the **Name** of the view to something appropriate, for example, **My Organization's Powered Off VMs**, and add information in the **Description** box to describe your changes.

3. Click on **4. Data** to expand that section.

4. Browse the metric tree for **Disk Space Reclamation | Reclaimable Capacity (GB)**.

5. Drag **Disk Space Reclamation | Reclaimable Capacity (GB)** to the center panel.

6. Provide a slightly shorter **Metric Label**.

7. Next, we will add a **Summary** field for our view, so click on the **Summary** tab.

8. Click on the *plus* icon to add the **summary** row.

9. Configure the **summary** row as follows:
   ° **Summary title**: Change the title to **Total**.
   ° **Aggregation**: Select **Sum** from the dropdown list as we want the total value for each data column.

10. Finally, click on **Save** to save your new view.

You can now browse to an object in your environment, such as **vSphere World**, and see the results of your new view.

Host, Datastore, and Cluster views

Some of the useful **Host**, **Datastore**, and **Cluster** views include the following:

• **Cluster Capacity Risk Forecast**: A list of clusters, showing how many Virtual Machines and Hosts they contain, and their forecasted capacity for 30, 60, and 90 days.

• **Datastore Inventory – Disk Space**: A list of all the datastores with metrics showing when they are projected to run out of space, their utilization, overcommit, and used template space.

- **Datastore Reclaimable Space**: A list of datastores showing the categorized reclaimable space. This is a particularly useful view, and I often see it used in dashboards.

- **Host Rightsizing CPU, Memory and Disk Space**: A list of Hosts summarizing the recommended CPU, memory, and disk space. The list is filtered to include only **Oversized** Hosts.

Capacity Projects

In the final part of this chapter on capacity planning, we will look at the new feature introduced into vRealize Operations 6 — **Capacity Projects**.

In the previous versions of vCenter Operations, there was the capability to perform a "What if" analysis with respect to capacity planning. The purpose was to help the administrator understand the impact on the capacity model of adding or removing workload or resources.

The principle was a good one; however, it was relatively inflexible, and the "What if" scenarios could not be saved or committed into the capacity plans.

The Capacity Projects capability is designed to overcome this weakness.

With Capacity Projects, you can take future known changes to your environment and apply them to your capacity model in order to understand if you are going to have a shortfall of capacity and where your capacity pinch points are.

You can additionally **Commit** these projects to your environment. This means that their impact is included in the **Days Remaining** dashboards and badges.

For example, you may know that there is a project coming down the line, where you are going to add 40 Virtual Machines of a particular size and utilization profile in two months' time.

You are also going to add two more Hosts to your cluster and some additional storage to support this workload. With the Capacity Projects functionality, you can understand how this is going to impact your environment.

Adding a Capacity Project

The Capacity Projects workspace is a tab accessible from every object's dashboard.

1. You navigate to **Capacity Projects** by selecting an object in your environment and clicking on the **Projects** tab.

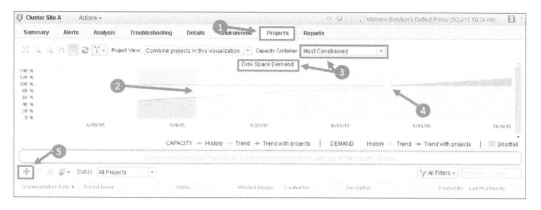

In the preceding example, we get a very good visualization of the capacity of one of our clusters. It shows us the following:

2. We currently have sufficient capacity for our workload. The top line represents useable capacity. The rising line shows the observed utilization and then the predicted capacity for the upcoming 90 days.

3. It visualizes our *most constrained* container or resource dimension. We can see that this is **Disk Space Demand**.

4. In about 50 days, we will reach capacity and there will be **shortfall**, which will be represented by red shading.

5. Now that we know we have a shortfall, let's add some storage capacity and see how that impacts our capacity model. Click on the green *plus* icon to add a Capacity Project.

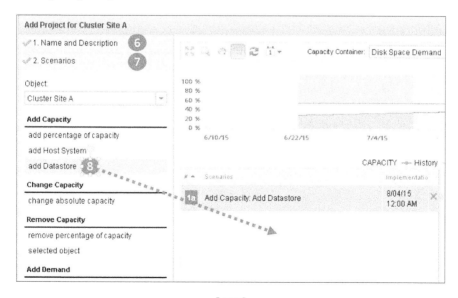

6. First, we need to give this Project a name — **Add Datastore**. We'll leave the status of the Project as **Planned – No badges affected** for now. Here, you could also select which badges out of Capacity Remaining and Time Remaining are affected.

7. Click on **2. Scenarios** to add our **Add Datastore** project.

8. Drag the **Add Datastore** scenario to the workspace.

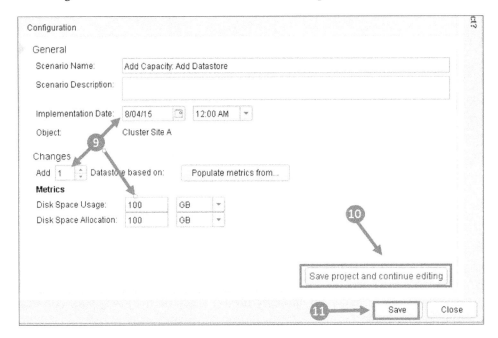

9. We can now configure the scenario:
    - **Implementation Date** – This is when we are going to implement the new datastore and make it available for use.
    - We are going to add one new datastore.
    - We set **Disk Space Usage** and **Disk Space Allocation** to 100 GB, the size of the datastore that we are going to add.

10. Click on **Save Project and Continue Editing** to add this scenario to the visualization in the top panel.

11. Finally, click on **Save** to save this project.

So far, this is just a draft or planned project. We would typically leave them as planned projects, while we model the proposed projects against our environment. Later on, when we know exactly which projects are going ahead, we can *commit* them and they will then be reflected in the capacity planning badges and dashboards.

To visualize this project in our **Projects** workspace, we need to drag it from the list of projects to the **Central Projects** bar.

We can now see, in the above visualization, that we are no longer constrained for capacity for the foreseeable future.

Multiple capacity projects can be combined to show the cumulative effect of the pipeline of projects that you may have in your organization. Let's now look at the impact of adding a new CRM system into our environment. We will add this as a second project.

As we did before, we initiate this by clicking on the green *Plus* icon and giving the project a name.

Instead of adding a datastore, this time I have dragged **Add Virtual Machine(s)** into the scenario panel. I have configured this as follows:

- **Implementation Date**: I have chosen a date after the implementation of the initial datastore that we added earlier.
- **Add 4** virtual machines with the following characteristics:
    ◦ **Memory 2GB Allocated**
    ◦ **CPU 1000 MHz**
    ◦ **Disk Space 10GB** (note that this is not visible in the preceding screenshot; you would need to scroll down to see it)

Clicking on **Save** adds this second project plan to our cluster.

Combining and committing Capacity Projects

Now that we have two Capacity Projects defined, we can look at how they can be combined.

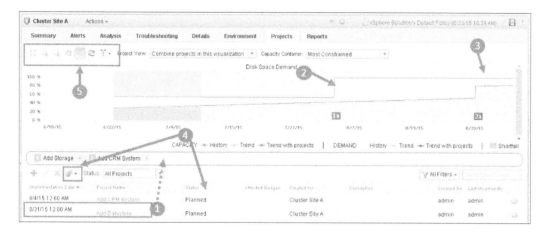

1. The first thing to do is to add the second project into the workspace by dragging it into the central bar.

2. Notice **1a** – The overall capacity available has increased as a result of adding the datastore.

3. Notice **2a** – The overall workload has increased as we add the CRM system. We can, however, still see that we are not yet constrained for capacity.

4. Assuming the projects are live and scheduled, we can click on the *Cog* icon and change the status of each project to **Committed**. This means that Capacity planning, trending, and reporting will reflect these known changes to the workload and resources in our environment.

5. Finally, there are some options in the top-left panel to zoom and pan the workspace as well as change the date range. In this particular case, I have changed the date range from the default of 60 days to 90 days.

Once the date for the capacity project has passed, the project is expired and no longer has an impact on the capacity planning badges, as it is assumed that the change has been made to the environment. There are no checks made by the system to confirm any changes have been made or that they were the same as the changes planned.

Other Capacity Project Visualizations

There are other ways in which you will visualize your Capacity Projects. In the example that we worked through above, we were always looking at the **Most Constrained** Resource Dimension or Capacity Container.

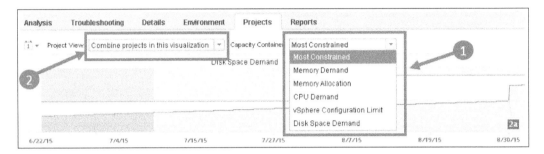

1. Selecting the dropdown, you can look at all your **Resource Dimensions** in turn. This will allow you to see whether there are other areas that you may want to address during a project.

   For example, **Disk Space** may be the most constrained; however, further analysis using this dropdown may reveal that **Memory Allocation** is also beginning to become constrained and may need addressing.

   > Most constrained means most constrained *today*. It is important to cycle through the other visualizations to see the cumulative impact.

2. We can also perform Capacity Comparisons. This will allow you to look at two, or more, different projects, and the impact that they would individually have on Capacity. This allows you to make decisions on, perhaps, alternate timing or resourcing of Projects.

Capacity Projects and days remaining

One of the key capabilities of Capacity Projects is the ability for **Committed** Capacity projects to have a bearing on the **Days Remaining** calculations.

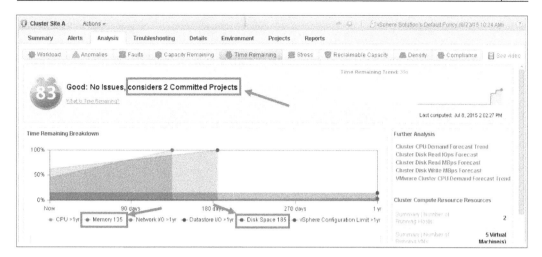

As you can see in the preceding screenshot, now that we have **committed** the two Capacity Projects, the Days Remaining dashboard reflects these projects.

Interestingly, in this example, you can also see that memory has become the Resource Dimension that will be out of capacity first, in 135 days. Disk space will be consumed in 185 days.

This shows the importance of using Days Remaining as the place to go when it comes to understanding the most important aspect of Capacity Planning — *"When am I going to run out of Capacity and which resource dimensions(s) will be impacted?"*

Summary

In this chapter, covering the capacity planning capabilities of vRealize Operations, we initially looked at the difference between Demand and Allocation capacity planning principles.

We then went on to look at how you can set your Default Policy to reflect your use of the Demand or Allocation models.

Next, we looked at the capacity planning Dashboards and Views, and how you can use them to visualize and understand the utilization of your environment.

Finally, we looked at how the Capacity Projects functionality can be used for planning for future known workload and resource changes.

In the next chapter, we will look at how you can extend the capabilities of vRealize Operations by adding Management Packs or Solutions.

7
vRealize Operations Manager Solutions

In this chapter, we will look at how vRealize Operations can be extended to manage more than just vSphere.

There is an ever expanding set of Solutions, or Management Packs, that can be downloaded and installed onto the vRealize Operations platform. These allow the vSphere Administrator to get the same insight, and management capabilities, with infrastructure and applications, that they do with the vSphere Solution we have been looking at so far.

We will show you where you can find the Management Packs, what comes with them, and how to install them.

Finally, in this chapter, we will also look at how you can use the PAK Manager to keep the vRealize Operations platform up to date.

Management Packs overview

The vRealize Operations platform has always been designed with extensibility in mind. With the release of vRealize Operations 6, there was a step change in the quantity, and quality, of **Management Packs** available. A lot of content, now an important part of vRealize Operations, is provided by and within the Management Packs.

 The terms **Solutions** and **Management Packs** are interchangeable in vRealize Operations. You will generally see them described as Solutions in the UI, and as Management Packs in Solutions Exchange, and much of the documentation. For the rest of this chapter, we will solely refer to them as Management Packs.

So far in this book, we have only used the vSphere Management Pack that is shipped with vRealize Operations. Although we didn't have to install it, if you watch the vRealize Operations installation carefully, you will see that it is a separate component that is installed during the vRealize Operations installation.

The vSphere Management Pack has been built to manage vSphere. The other Management Packs available to you have been built to manage other parts of your environment. For example, there are Management Packs available to manage your storage arrays, applications such as Oracle, or SAP, operating systems or networking technologies such as VMware NSX.

At the time of writing, there were 77 Management Packs available on VMware's **Solution Exchange** website. I spend a lot of my time on Solutions Exchange, and it seems that every time I visit there is another Management Pack available.

Apart from extending vRealize Operations to manage other (non-vSphere) parts of your environment, the Management Packs work together by taking advantage of the relationships, and hierarchical tree traversal capability in vRealize Operations.

For example, when managing vSphere, you can see in the **Environment** dashboard in the UI, that VMs have a hierarchical relationship with the other Object Types such as Host Systems, Cluster Compute Resources, and Datastores.

If you add, say, a storage Management Pack, further relationships will be built to allow you to see the relationship between your Datastores and storage Object Types such as LUNs and RAID Groups. This is critical when troubleshooting issues that manifest themselves up and down the stack.

Management Pack types and entitlement

The use of Management Packs is governed by the terms of the vRealize Operations EULA. We looked at the different editions of vRealize Operations in *Chapter 1, Introduction to vRealize Operations Manager*. It is the edition of vRealize Operations you have, that will determine which Management Packs you are **entitled** to install.

There are three main types of Management Packs:

- **Advanced Management Packs**: These are the most commonly used packs and can be installed if you have the Advanced or Enterprise Editions of vRealize Operations. These packs are built to manage your infrastructure components such as Storage, Networks, and Operating Systems.
- **Enterprise Management Packs**: These are available to you if you have the Enterprise Edition of vRealize Operations. They are designed to manage your in-guest applications such as Oracle, Microsoft SQL, and SAP.

- **Extensibility Tools**: This is where a Management Pack does not exist for something you want to manage and monitor within vRealize Operations. There are extensibility packs which can collect time serialized data from sources such as HTTP, SQL, or Text. You will need the Advanced or Enterprise editions of vRealize Operations to use these.

There are also different publishers of Management Packs as follows:

- **VMware Management Packs**: These are built and supported by VMware and are provided at no extra charge above the regular license fee for vRealize Operations. The exceptions to this are the Health Care focused Management Packs for EPIC and MEDITECH for which VMware charge an additional license fee.

- **Partner Management Packs**: These are built and supported by either the manufacturer of the object being managed or by a third-party partner such as Blue Medora. For example, the Management Packs for Hitachi storage are written by Hitachi, whereas the NetApp Management Pack is written by Blue Medora.

  Partner Management Packs are not included with the vRealize Operations license. Some partners may charge an extra license fee and others may include the Management Pack as part of their their product.

 The Management Pack marketplace changes very frequently, so VMware maintains a whitepaper with all the latest information. This can be found at www.vmware.com/go/management-packs.

Management Pack content

When extensibility was first introduced into vCenter Operations, the only thing initially provided was an **adapter**. This adapter was a piece of code that would connect to the object to be managed and collect metric data.

Over time, this has improved substantially and Management Packs now have the following capabilities built in:

- **Adapters**: There is still an adapter in the Management Pack. This will generally connect to the management interface of an object type to be managed. For example, HP's Storefront Analytics Management Pack connects to HP 3PAR or HP StoreVirtual systems.

  The adapter collects **metrics**, **properties**, and **events** at a regular interval, usually every 5 minutes. The adapter also collects the information required to allow vRealize Operations to understand the relationships between different object types from different Management Packs.

Not all adapters are collectors. In some cases, the object being managed will push the metrics and properties to the vRealize Operations cluster. An example of this is vRealize Operations for Horizon. While the vRealize Operations for Horizon adapter collects data from the Horizon brokers, the VDI desktops themselves send information using the installed Horizon agent.

- **Dashboards**: A Management Pack will typically install one or more Custom Dashboards. These are created by the Management Pack author to provide rich visualizations of the objects being managed.

  These Dashboards are no different to the ones you could create yourself using the custom dashboards' capability. However, as the Management Pack author intimately knows the product being managed and also understands the troubleshooting flow and steps to be followed, these dashboards are very effective.

- **Views and reports**: Apart from Content in the form of Dashboards, the Management Pack will create some Views and Report templates for you to use.

- **Alerts, Symptoms, Recommendations, and Actions**: This is the final bit of Content that the Management Pack will install. Again, the Management Pack author will know the best practices for monitoring their devices, so will create Symptoms, Recommendations, and Actions that follow those best practices.

  For example, the Management Pack for NSX has Alert Definitions that check for things such as incorrectly configured NSX Controllers and mismatched MTU sizes.

- **Object Types and Base Settings**: A Management pack will typically create additional Object Types, and these will all come with predefined Base Settings.

- **Capacity Model**: All of the new Object Types can have a Capacity Model defined for them. This will define the dimensions through which the capacity for an Object Type is considered, how Capacity will be calculated for these dimensions, and any settings that will be user customizable through Policy changes.

The Management Packs are provided as .PAK files. These contain all the scripts for installation and make installation and configuration of Management Packs a very simple process.

Solution Exchange

Extensibility content for all of VMware's management products is available on their Solution Exchange website at `http://solutionexchange.vmware.com`.

As can be seen in the preceding screenshot, VMware Solution Exchange is grouped by product. Selecting **vRealize Operations Management** will bring up all the available vRealize Operations Management Packs.

The Management Packs are then subsequently grouped into the following:

- **Extensibility Tools**: These are the Management Packs that allow you to manage objects where there is not a Management Pack already built.

> The Extensibility Tools are generally fairly complex to install and configure – if you do have the requirement to collect data from objects, for which there is not an out of the box Management Pack, it is likely that you will need to engage VMware's Professional Services Organization (PSO) to help with the integration work.

- **Advanced Management Packs**: These are for installation on the Advanced Edition of vRealize Operations.

- **Enterprise Management Pack**: These are for installation on the Enterprise Edition of vRealize Operations.

Solution Exchange contains information about the Management Packs and links to documentation and the code itself. In cases where a third-party partner is supplying the Management Pack, Solution Exchange will generally provide a link directly to that partner.

Installing Management Packs

Installing Management Packs is a very straightforward exercise. This makes it very easy for you to extend your vRealize Operations solution to manage other parts of your environment such as your storage arrays, applications, or networking technologies, such as VMware NSX.

Let's look at how you install a Management Pack. We will use the **Management Pack for NSX for vSphere 2.0** as our example. This is very typical of the Management Packs created by VMware.

Downloading the Management Pack code and documentation

The first thing to do is to browse to VMware's Solution Exchange, as described earlier, to locate the Management Pack you want to install. Browse through the Management Packs to locate the one you are interested in, or alternatively, use the **Search** functionality.

Each Management Pack has a short description as can be seen in the following screenshot:

Once you have located the Management Pack, clicking on it will take you to its page on Solution Exchange. Here you will find everything you need for understanding and using the Management Pack.

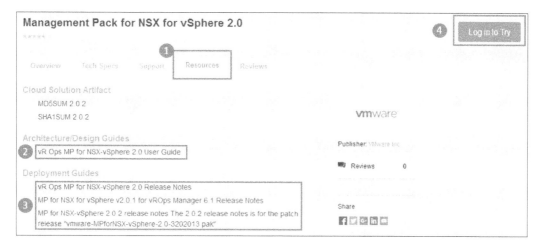

1. First, click on the **Resources** tab to see the resources that are available.

2. It's always worth checking the **Release Notes** for up-to-date information on the Management Pack. This will often describe the specific versions of vRealize Operations that are supported by the Management Pack in question.

3. There will be a user guide that will describe installation, and the Management Pack itself. The User Guide will often contain details on the metrics and properties being collected and may describe the Capacity Model for the new Object Types installed.

4. Finally, click on **Login to Try** to gain access to the .PAK file. If you do not have an account on Solution Exchange, you can register at this point.

   The .PAK file for the selected Management Pack will be downloaded.

Installing the Management Pack

Now, we will install the Management Pack on the vRealize Operations cluster:

1. Click on the **Administration** icon. The Administration dashboard will default to **Solutions**.

2. Click on the green **Plus** icon to add a new Management Pack as shown in the preceding screenshot.

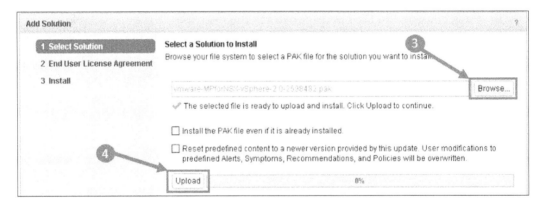

3. In the **Add Solution** dialog box, click on **Browse** to locate the .PAK file you downloaded from Solution Exchange.

There are two other options you can select in this panel:

Install the PAK file even if it is already installed. Use this if you need to re-install the Management Pack.

Reset predefined content: If you have made changes to Alerts, Symptoms, Recommendations, or Policies for the Management Pack and are reinstalling it, checking this box will overwrite these changes.

It is best practice to always clone Content rather than changing it. If you follow this practice, then you will always be able to check this box safe in the knowledge that your cloned content will not be overwritten.

4. Click on **Upload** to upload the code to the vRealize Operations cluster.

5. Once uploaded, click on **Next** to move to the EULA.

With the release of vRealize Operations 6.1, Management Packs have had the option to be digitally signed. Not all packs have had this option enabled, so, at this point, you may be warned that the Management Pack is unsigned with a prompt asking if you wish to continue.

6. If required, accept the EULA and click on **Next**.

The PAK file will be installed.

7. Once complete, click on **Finish**.

If you don't click on **Finish**, the installation will not be set to complete. This sometimes happens if you start an install and leave it for too long. The UI may timeout and log you out. If that happens, you may need to start the install again, but may need to tick the **Install the PAK file even if it is already installed** checkbox before step 4 that we saw earlier.

8. The Management Pack you just installed will now appear in the list of Solutions. All that is left now is to configure it.

9. The final step will be to click on the Cog icon to configure the solution.

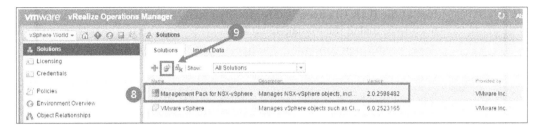

How you configure the Management Pack will vary from solution to solution, and will generally be described very well in the documentation from Solution Exchange. As the NSX MP is typical of most Management Packs, let's look at the configuration options for this Management Pack.

Once you click on the Cog icon as described earlier, the following configuration panel will appear:

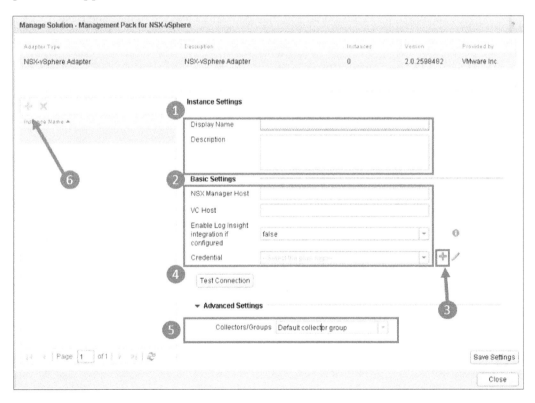

When you configure the Management Pack, you are generally creating one or more adapters that connect from the vRealize Operations cluster to the object(s) being managed. The adapter will have the following typical elements for configuration:

1. **Adapter Settings**: These are settings that describe the adapter itself. They consist of the following:

    ° **Display Name**: This is a label to give the adapter. This will become the name of the adapter object within vRealize Operations.

    ° **Description**: This is free form text to describe the adapter.

2. **Basic Settings**: This is where you configure what the adapter is connecting to and the credentials to be used:

    ° **Management targets**: One or more systems that the adapter will connect to, in order to collect metrics and properties. In this case, the NSX Management Pack connects to an NSX Manager Host and a vCenter Server.

    ° **Other settings**: Some Management Packs will have additional integration settings. In this case, there is the option to configure Log Insight integration.

    ° **Credential**: To connect to an external source, you will need a credential.

3. To add a credential, use the green *plus* arrow.

There isn't a central credentials database. Each Management Pack has its own set of credentials.

4. The **Test Connection** button will test the settings in Basic Settings and confirm you have everything configured correctly.

Test Connection will sometimes fail even though you have configured the correct FQDN for the object being managed and its credentials. You may even get a certificate back, which suggests that the connectivity is fine.

One of the most common reasons I come across for being unable to configure adapters, is incorrectly configured **DNS**.

It is important that you configure both **forward** and **reverse** looking entries for DNS for all your vRealize Operations nodes and for the objects being managed.

5. **Advanced Settings**: These will be optional settings. There is usually the option to change **Collectors** or **Collector Groups** that the adapter will be installed on. Selecting **Default Collector Group** will usually be fine; however, if you want to place the adapter on a specific node, you can select that here.

6. Finally, once you have configured an adapter, you can add further **instances** of the adapter, connecting to other Management sources, by clicking on the green *plus* icon.

Upgrading vRealize Operations

VMware releases regular minor, and major, versions of vRealize Operations. We will look at installing these updates in this section.

In general, the upgrades are a fairly straightforward task, involving the installation of a PAK file and, occasionally, an OS upgrade.

The upgrade from v6.0.3 to v6.1 is very typical, so let's step through it now.

Upgrading from vCenter Operations 5.8.x is not nearly as straightforward as the vRealize Operations upgrade from v6.03 to v6.1 described later.

The upgrade from vCenter Operations is, in fact, a side-by-side migration. You start by installing a vRealize Operations 6.0.3 cluster and then use the Installation Wizard to **migrate** from vCenter Operations 5.8.x. Full instructions are provided in the installation documentation; however, if you have a complex implementation, I recommend engaging VMware's Professional Services Organisation (PSO) to assist.

There is no direct upgrade path from v5.8.x to v6.1 or higher. You first need to migrate to v6.0.3 and then perform a regular in place upgrade to v6.1 or higher.

Upgrade Code and Release Notes

The first place to look at is the **Release Notes** for the version of vRealize Operations you will upgrade to. The Release Notes will highlight the process for the upgrade, and include information on the fixes and new capability in the new version. They will also highlight existing known issues, so they are a really valuable source of information.

The code itself will be available for download from your My VMware account. The Release Notes will highlight the components you need to download.

 As with most VMware products, entitlement to updated versions of the vRealize Operations software is dependent on having a **Software and Support** (**SnS**) contract in place.

In the case of upgrading to version 6.1 of the appliance, the following components are required:

- **vRealize_Operations_Manager-VA-OS-xxx.pak**: This is an OS upgrade for the underlying operating system for your cluster node(s).
- **vRealize_Operations_Manager-VA-xxx.pak**: This is the vRealize code itself

The Release Notes, in this particular case, advise to update the OS first, and then the vRealize Operations code itself.

Performing the upgrade

The upgrade is carried out in the **Administrator UI** of your **Master Node**. To access this, browse to `https://FQDNofMasterNode/admin`.

You will need to use the **admin** account of vRealize Operations to log in.

Before you start, I would always advise you perform a **snapshot** of the nodes in your cluster.

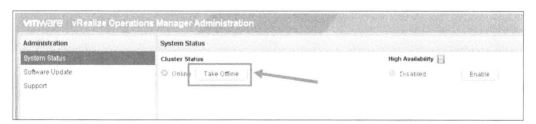

If it is a multi-node cluster, you should:

- Take the cluster offline as shown in the preceding screenshot.
- Shut down the individual cluster nodes using their console or using the vSphere Client.
- Take your snapshot(s) in the vSphere client.

- Restart the cluster nodes. These do not need to be restarted in any particular order.

- Once all the cluster nodes have restarted, take the Cluster online in the Administrator UI.

Another thing worth doing is to increase your inactivity timeout while you perform the upgrade. The default is 30 minutes; however, some of the steps can be quite lengthy, and I often find myself getting distracted and my session times out. It can sometimes be awkward to restart the upgrade, so I prefer not to time out.

You can change this setting by navigating to **Administration | Global Settings** then edit the **Session Timeout** value. A value of **120 minutes** usually works for me.

Once you are ready to start the upgrade, the steps to follow are as shown in the following screenshots:

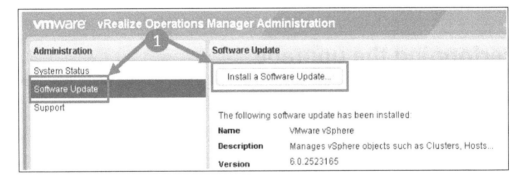

1. Click on **Software Update** and select **Install a Software Update**.
2. Click on **Browse** and then locate the **OS update PAK** file and click on **Open**.
3. Click on **Upload** to upload the code to the appliance.

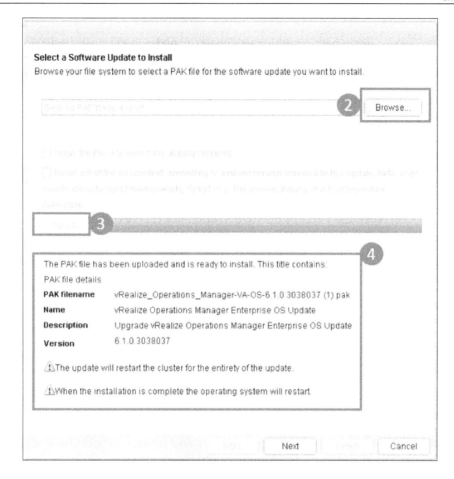

4. Once uploaded, you will get confirmation of the upload and will be advised that the update will restart the cluster and the node operating systems. Click on **Next** to continue.

   It may take a while for the preceding dialog box to appear—the staging process does not have a progress bar, so it may appear to have hung. It will be OK, just be patient!

5. Check the EULA acceptance box and click on **Next**.

6. The OS upgrade will now be installed. This might take 30 minutes or more, but you will see regular updates in the dialog box.

7. Once this step is complete, the cluster will be restarted and you will be logged out. When you log in again to the Administrator UI, and navigate to **Software Update**, you will see the upgrade is completed.

If you have a multi-node cluster, all nodes in the cluster will be updated by this process.

8. Now, we need to upgrade the vRealize Operations code itself. Click on **Install a Software Update** again and follow the same process as we did for the OS upgrade.

9. Browse for the **vRealize Operations PAK** file.

10. Click on **Upload** to upload the code. Again, this may take a while and seem to pause at the staging step.

11. Click on **Next**, then accept the EULA, and click on **Next** to initiate the upgrade.

12. As before, the progress of the upgrade can be monitored in the dialog box and you will be logged out once complete.

Not all upgrades will require an OS upgrade but the above is very typical of the upgrade experience with vRealize Operations. Compared with some other products, you should find it very easy to keep your installation up to date.

Summary

In this chapter, we looked at how vRealize Operations can be extended with the addition of Management Packs.

We covered the make up of a Management Pack and looked at Solution Exchange where you can get access to all the Management Packs you may need.

Finally, we looked at how you can keep your vRealize Operations up to date with the latest code available from VMware.

In the next chapter, we will look at one of the key adjacencies of vRealize Operations, vRealize Infrastructure Navigator.

8
vRealize Infrastructure Navigator

Until now, we have concentrated on functionality within vRealize Operations Manager. In this chapter, we will look at how you can extend the capabilities of vRealize Operations with the implementation of vRealize Infrastructure Navigator.

We will look at the following topics in this chapter:

- Deployment and configuration of the Virtual Infrastructure Navigator appliance, and then the integration with vRealize Operations through its Management Pack.

- Dependency mapping: This covers how dependencies between VMs are created through the definition, and mapping, of applications.

- Grouping: This covers how interconnected Virtual Machines can be grouped into applications and services.

- Integrations with vRealize Operations Manager: This is how the applications and services can be surfaced and managed within vRealize Operations.

Introduction to vRealize Infrastructure Navigator

vRealize Infrastructure Navigator is a component of the Advanced and Enterprise Editions of the vRealize Operations Management suite.

The solution enables the administrator to:

- **Discover** and **map** dependencies and relationships between Virtual Machines.

- Understand the applications that are running on Virtual Machines and the TCP/UDP ports through which they communicate.

- **Group** related VMs together, either automatically or manually, to create applications and services that can be managed and visualized as a single entity in vRealize Operations.

- Determine whether all Virtual Machines in a group are protected by VMware vCenter **Site Recovery Manager** (**SRM**) and, if so, whether they are in the same SRM Recovery Group.

Architecture

I often think of vRealize Infrastructure Navigator as an **extension** to vSphere, to provide the additional functionality listed in the previous section.

The solution is installed as a virtual appliance and is connected to a vCenter Server. The virtual appliance collects information from vCenter regarding the applications and services running on the hosted Virtual Machines and the TCP/UDP ports through which these applications, and services communicate.

This information is gathered directly from the Virtual Machines by **VMware Tools**, using the **VIX API**.

 There is a one-to-one mapping of Virtual Infrastructure Navigator appliance to vCenter. You will need to install one appliance for every vCenter that you have.

An illustration of the entire technical architecture can be seen from the following screenshot, taken from the Virtual Infrastructure Navigator's online help documentation:

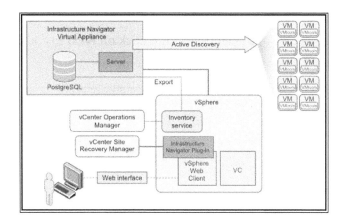

Deployment

The Virtual Infrastructure Navigator virtual appliance is deployed using the vSphere Web Client. You will gain access to the appliance in the OVF form if you are entitled to the Advanced, or Enterprise Editions of vRealize Operations, or if you have registered for a vRealize Operations evaluation.

To deploy the appliance, follow these steps:

1. In the vSphere web client, right-click on the cluster or datacenter in which you want to deploy the virtual appliance, and select **Deploy OVF Template** to start the deployment wizard.

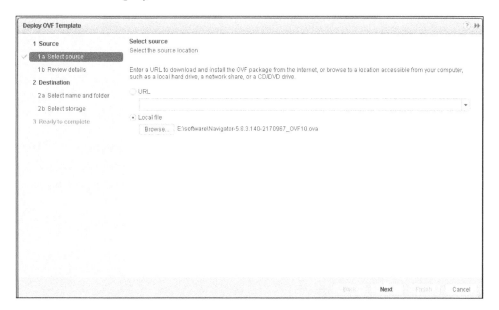

2. Browse for the installation **OVF** file, and click on **Next** to continue.

3. Review the details of the template, and click on **Next** to continue.

4. Accept the EULA, and click on **Next** to continue.

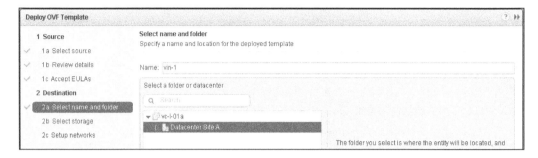

5. Provide a **Name** for your virtual appliance, and then select a **folder** or **datacenter,** in which to deploy it. Click on **Next** to continue.

6. Select a datastore with sufficient capacity, and choose the virtual disk **format**. Thin provisioning is fine for this appliance — it will require 2 GB if thin provisioned, and 20 GB if thick provisioned. Click on **Next** to continue.

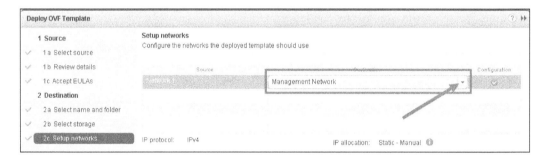

7. Using the dropdown shown in the preceding screenshot, select the network on which you want the virtual appliance deployed, and click on **Next** to continue. The appliance needs to be on a network with connectivity to the vCenter server it will be paired with and your vRealize Operations cluster.

With the increase in the number of management devices for virtual infrastructure, I often see a dedicated network in place to support them.

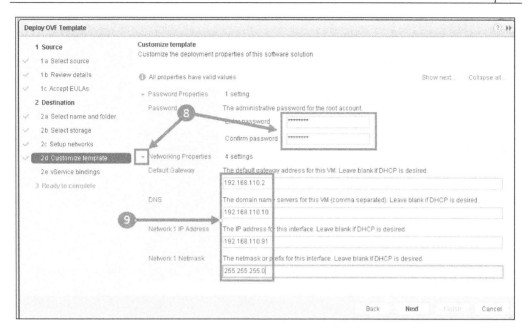

8. Enter and confirm a **password** for the virtual appliance's root account, and then, click on the **arrow** to expand the **Networking Properties** section.

9. In the Networking Properties section, complete the following fields for your virtual appliance, then click on **Next** to continue:

   ° **Default Gateway**
   ° **DNS Server(s)** – comma separated
   ° **IP Address**
   ° **Netmask**

 If you don't enter the Networking Properties, a DHCP address will be used, if available, for the virtual appliance. I recommend using static IP addresses.

10. Click on **Next** to confirm the vService bindings.

11. Optionally, tick the **Power on after deployment** checkbox, and click on **Finish** to complete the wizard, and install the virtual appliance.

Configuring vRealize infrastructure navigator

Once the virtual appliance is deployed and has started up, we need to license it, connect it to its vCenter, and complete the configuration.

Licensing the appliance

1. In the vSphere Web Client, select **Home**, and then **Licensing**.

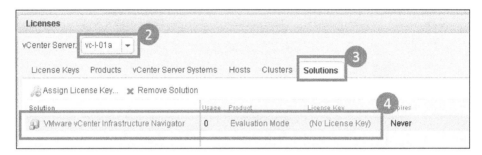

2. Choose the **vCenter server** hosting the appliance from the dropdown list of vCenters.

3. Click on the **Solutions** tab.

4. Click on the **vRealize Infrastructure Navigator** appliance that does not have a license assigned.

5. Assign your license key to the appliance and click on **OK**.

Configuring the appliance

1. In the vSphere Web Client, select **Home** and then **Infrastructure Navigator**.

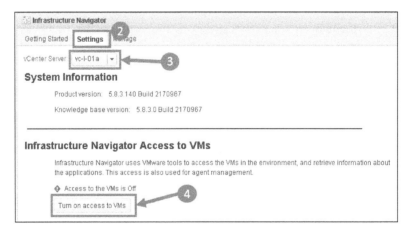

2. Select the **Settings** tab.

3. Use the dropdown to select the **vCenter** with which you want to pair this vRealize Infrastructure Navigator appliance.

4. Click on **Turn on access to VMs**. In the dialogue box that opens, enter credentials with the required permissions to access the VMs hosted by the vCenter.

   In general, you would use an administrative account; however, this could be considered a security risk so you can create an account with the minimal permissions required. This would be a vCenter role with the permissions:

   ° **Virtual Machine | Interaction | Guest operating system management by VIX API** and **Console interaction**.

5. Click on **OK** to complete the configuration.

Virtual Infrastructure Navigator is now installed and configured. It will perform an initial discovery, and will subsequently run additional discoveries every hour.

Installing the Management Pack for vRealize Infrastructure Navigator

The final installation step is the integration with vRealize Operations. This will allow you, within the vRealize Operations UI, to consume the applications, and metadata, discovered by vRealize Infrastructure Navigator.

As discussed in the previous chapter, Management Packs are downloadable from http://solutionexchange.vmware.com.

Once you have downloaded the Management Pack, it is installed as follows:

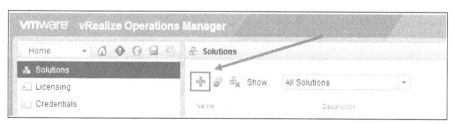

1. Navigate to **Administration | Solutions** and click on the *plus* icon to start installation.

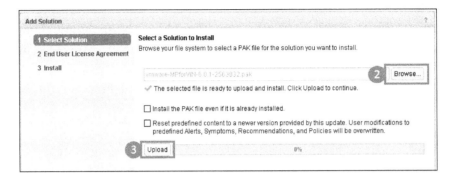

2. Click on **Browse**, to locate the PAK file you downloaded from Solution Exchange.

3. Click on **Upload** to start the installation.

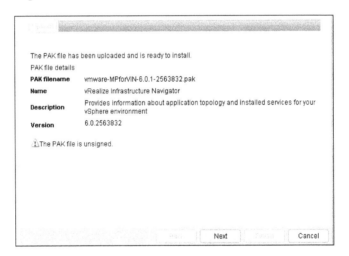

4. Once the PAK file is uploaded and ready to install, click on **Next** to continue.

5. Accept the EULA, and click on **Next** to continue.

6. Once installed, click on **Finish** to complete the installation wizard.

7. Now click on the *cog* icon to configure the Management Pack.

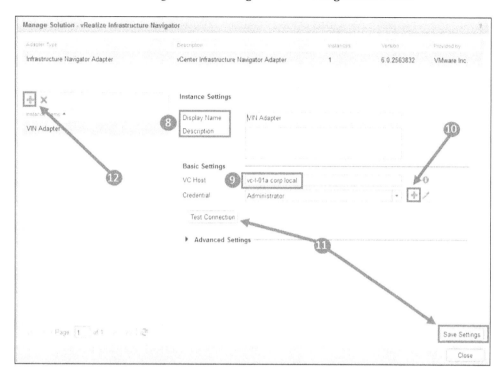

8. Provide a **Display Name** and **Description** for the adapter.

9. Enter the **FQDN** of the vCenter that your Virtual Infrastructure Navigator appliance is to be paired with.

10. Click on the *plus* icon to add a **credential** for connectivity to your vCenter. This account will need the same permissions as the vSphere solution that we installed in *Chapter 2, Install, Configure, and Administer vRealize Operations Manager.*

11. Click on **Test Connection** to ensure everything is entered correctly, and then click on **Save Settings**.

12. If you have further vCenter and vRealize Infrastructure Navigator appliance pairs, click on the *plus* icon in the left hand panel to add additional adapter instances.

13. Finally, click on **Close** to close the configuration panel.

Using vRealize Infrastructure Navigator

Now that we have deployed and configured the solution, let's take a look at how the solution can be used to map **applications** and **dependencies**, and feed these into vRealize Operations.

The two key constructs that you will use, to gain insight into the applications and dependencies in your environment are:

- **Service definitions**.
- **Application definitions**.

Service definitions

The vRealize Infrastructure Navigator solution uses **VMware Tools** on Virtual Machines to discover the applications and processes that are running, and the ports through which they are communicating.

Many of the commonly used applications, such as Microsoft SQL and Apache Tomcat, have predefined **Service Definitions** within vRealize Infrastructure Navigator and, therefore, will be automatically discovered in your environment.

When vRealize Infrastructure Navigator discovers Virtual Machines with known Service Definitions, it can start to map how these Virtual Machines are communicating with each other, and you can start to build up maps, that represent your applications.

For example, for a traditional three-tier application, Virtual Infrastructure Navigator might see Microsoft IIS communicating with a JBoss Application Server, which in turn, might be communicating with a Microsoft SQL Server. You would then be able to group these together, and manage them as a single entity.

There will probably be cases where an out-of-the-box Service Definition does not exist for some of your applications. In these cases, you can create your own **custom** service definition.

The lab environment I set up for this book, has an instance of vRealize Log Insight installed, monitoring logs from all the servers in the environment. Out-of-the-box, vRealize Infrastructure Navigator does not recognize the Java processes that listen for incoming logs, so we can't immediately visualize, or map, these communications.

Let's take a look at this, and how we can create a custom Service Definition for a new, or unknown, application.

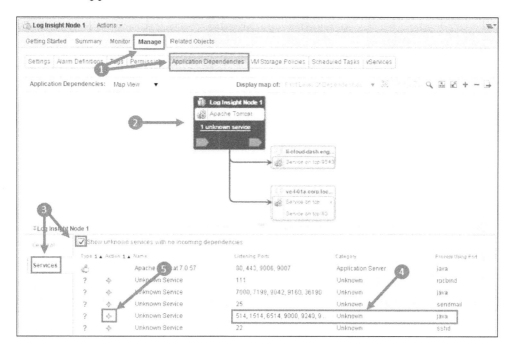

1. In the **vSphere Web Client**, we've navigated to the Log Insight Virtual Machine and then to **Manage | Application Dependencies**.

2. We can see the Log Insight Virtual Machine is highlighted, and it has outgoing connections to two other machines. One is the vCenter to which it is sending configuration information, the other, is a server in VMware, to which the solution is sending engineering feedback.

3. Clicking on the **Services** tab in the lower panel, then ticking **Show unknown services with no incoming dependencies** will show all the services running on this Virtual Machine.

4. We can see there is a Java service listening on a number of ports, including ports 514 and 9000, which are two of the ports used for log injection by Log Insight. Port 514 is used by Syslog and port 9000 is used for ingestion of Log Insight Windows agent logs.

5. As we know this service is for log ingestion on those ports; we can define a new **Service Definition** for this by clicking on the *plus* icon.

6. We configure the dialogue box as follows:

   ○ Ticking the **Process** and **Port** checkboxes ensures the Service Definition uses **both** the **process**, and **port(s)** used by that process to define the service.

   If just the port was ticked, then the Service Definition would be defined against every process listening on that port.

   This might misidentify services unnecessarily. For example, ports 80 and 443 are very widely used. If one of these were the port identified, and you only looked for this, and not the associated process, you will end up with a lot of dependencies identified solely on the basis of traffic on port 80 or 433.

   Although this would help identify dependencies between Virtual Machines, it won't provide enough detail on the applications communicating, for you to fully understand the services.

   The only time when we might do this would be for services external to the vCenter. In these cases, we have no visibility of the process name so it cannot be used as a basis for the Service Definition.

 You will notice only one port is shown in the dialogue box. If we select the process and port then **all** ports associated with that process will be associated with the Service Definition.

- ° We create a name to describe the service definition, in this case **Log Insight log ingestion**, and a category, in this case **Virtualization Management**, is selected from the dropdown.
- ° Clicking on **OK** saves the service definition.

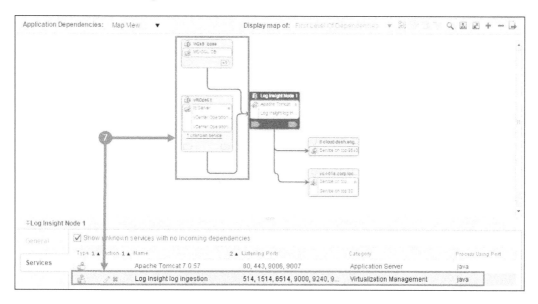

- ° Now, we can see two devices that are sending logs to that Java process on the Log Insight Virtual Machine. Any other devices sending logs will also be automatically discovered.

Once all our services are defined and the application dependencies are discovered, we can start to group sets of Virtual Machines together into applications.

Application definitions

An application definition can be thought of as one or more Virtual Machines with a set of specific services running on them.

For example, using our preceding Service Definitions, we might have a three-tier application that can be described with the following pattern:

- A **Web server** running Microsoft IIS
- An **Application** server running JBoss
- A **Database** server running Microsoft SQL Server

We can define these three tiers as an Application Definition within vRealize Infrastructure Navigator. Once defined, all discovered instances of this pattern will be grouped together as applications. We create this Application Definition as follows:

1. In the vSphere Web Client, navigate to **Home | Infrastructure Navigator**.

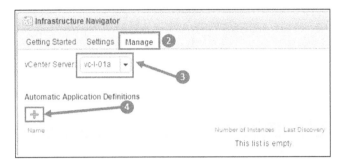

2. Click on the **Manage** tab.

3. Select the **vCenter** on which the Virtual Machines hosting the application exist.

4. Click on the *plus* icon to add an application definition.

5. The **Create Automatic Application Definition** wizard will start. Give your application a name, for example, **3-Tier Application**, and click on **Next**.

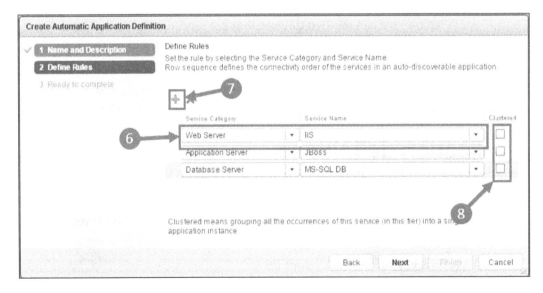

6. For each of the tiers, in turn, select the **Service Category** and **Service Name** that matches the processes or applications you are seeking to match. In the preceding example, these are:

   ° **Web Server – IIS**

   ° **Application Server – Jboss**

   ° **Database Server – MS_SQL DB**

7. Use the *plus* icon to add the second, and then, third tier.

8. In this case, we will uncheck the **clustered** checkbox. If it is checked, then all instances of the service will be grouped into a single Application Definition. If, say, you had four instances of this three-tiered application, you would end up with a single application consisting of four web, application, and database servers instead of four separate instances of the three-tiered application.

9. Click on **Next**, then **Finish** to complete the Application Definition.

10. Within a few minutes, you will see the discovered instances of the Application Definition, as in the preceding screenshot, where you can see two instances of the three-tier application.

Manual application definition

In some cases, it's not possible, or practical, to automate the creation of all your applications. For example, we might want the Log Insight server, referred to earlier, specifically related to our vRealize Operations servers.

If we created an Application Definition using the log ingestion service definition we used earlier, our automatically created application would encompass everything sending logs to Log Insight. This isn't necessarily what we want to happen.

In this case we could, alternatively, create a manual application as follows:

1. We've browsed to the Log Insight Virtual Machine in the vSphere Web Client and navigated to **Manage | Application Dependencies**.

2. Click on the create application icon to open the create application panel.

3. Provide a name, for example, **My Management Servers**, and click on **OK**.

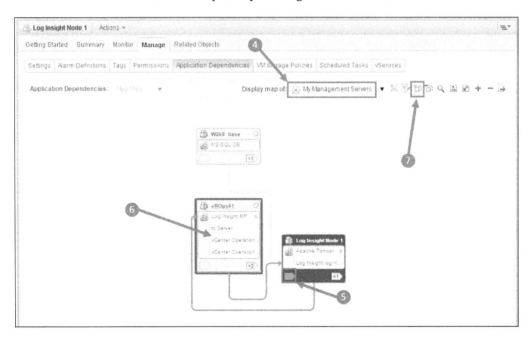

4. Now that we have the new manual application created, application dependencies, in this panel in vSphere Web Client, can be set to different **Application** contexts.

   We need to change the context from the default of **First Level of Dependencies** to the **My Management Servers** application we just created, using the dropdown.

5. Expand the visualization of **incoming dependencies** by clicking on the incoming dependency **arrow**.

6. Select the **server** to add to the Manual Application by clicking on it. In this case, we add the vRealize Operations server.

7. Click on the **Add selected application members** icon to complete the addition.

   When the screen refreshes, you will see the two members of the new manual application group.

Applications in vRealize Operations

Now that the applications in your environment have been mapped, and Virtual Machines grouped together, they are surfaced in vRealize Operations as a new object type, **Application Group**.

As well as these Application Group constructs, a lot of the metadata from vRealize Infrastructure Navigator is also added to Virtual Machines, so can be used throughout the vRealize Operations solution.

Application Group Objects

You can view your Application Group objects by navigating to **Environment |
Custom Groups**. You will see a new **Application Group** folder, which you can
expand to see your defined applications as shown in the following screenshot:

These Application Groups work in exactly the same way as the Custom Groups
we worked with in *Chapter 2, Install, Configure, and Administer vRealize Operations
Manager*, with the exception that they are created, and destroyed, **automatically**
based on data collection from vRealize Infrastructure Navigator.

If new applications are discovered they will automatically appear—similarly, if they
no longer exist, they will be deleted. Historical data for those group objects will also
be deleted depending on the data retention settings within vRealize Operations for
deleted objects.

Virtual Machine metadata

As well as surfacing new objects in vRealize Operations, additional properties will be
added to your Virtual Machines.

I often use these properties to create my own additional **Custom Groups**. For
example, I might want to create a Custom Group for all my Microsoft SQL servers,
so I can offer up dashboards to my SQL DBAs.

This is how you would use the properties surfaced by vRealize Infrastructure Navigator to do this:

1. Within vRealize Operations, navigate to **Environment | Custom Groups**, and click on the *plus* icon to add a new group.

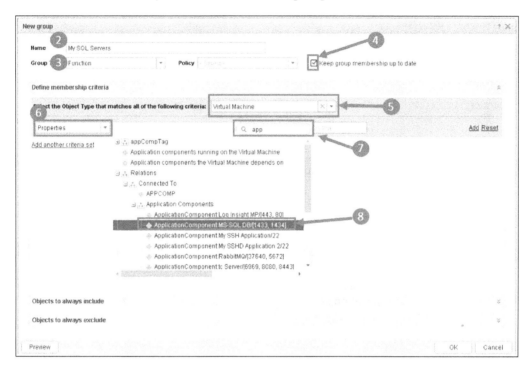

2. Provide a meaningful name for your group—**My SQL Servers**.

3. Select a **Group** folder—**Function**. Optionally, you can also select a **Policy** to assign to this group.

4. Tick the **Keep group membership up to date** checkbox. This means any new SQL Virtual Machines that appear in the environment will be automatically added to this group.

5. Use the Object Type selector to navigate to **vCenter Adapter | Virtual Machine** as the context for this group.

6. In the Criteria type dropdown, select **Properties** and click on **Pick a Property**.

7. The Properties tree will appear. At this point, I usually find it useful to use a filter. Using the text filter app will filter for this purpose nicely.

8. Expand the Properties tree and navigate to **Relations | Connected To | Application Components**.

   If you have SQL servers discovered, you will see a **ApplicationComponent:MS-SQL DB/[1433, 1434]** property to select.

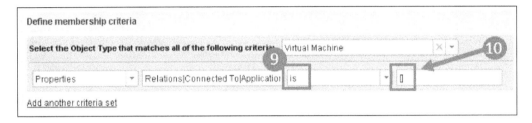

9. Select **is** as the operator.

10. In the value field enter [] (an opening and closing bracket).

11. Finally, click on **OK** to save the new group.

This is not the only way to achieve this—you could also have navigated to the property **appCompTag | Application components running on the Virtual Machine** with the operator **Contains MS-SQL DB**.

Both methods are equally valid—the first method is looking for a specific application and the TCP/UDP port pair, whereas the second is looking for a more generic text string.

Once you have your groups in place, you can use them as a dynamic basis for Views, Reports, Alerts, Policies, and many other features of vRealize Operations.

vRealize Infrastructure Navigator dashboards

The final integration point with vRealize Operations are the two dashboards that are created during the installation of the Management Pack.

The VIN Application Topology dashboard

This is reached by navigating to **Home | Dashboard List | VIN | VIN Application Topology**. The focus of the dashboard is your list of applications, and it has the following features:

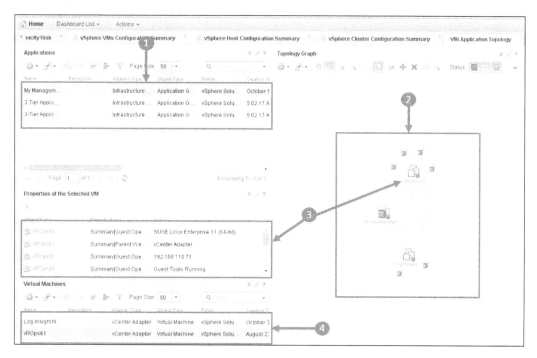

1. The dashboard context is created by selecting one of your applications in the **Applications** panel.

2. A visualization of the **Topology** of the selected application is shown in the right hand panel.

    Each Virtual Machine in this panel is surrounded by installed, and discovered, applications/services. Connected applications are visualized with connectors.

3. Selecting a Virtual Machine in the **Topology** panel populates the panel on the left with the list of discovered applications on that Virtual Machine.

4. The **Virtual Machines** panel, at the bottom of the dashboard, is populated with the Virtual Machines defined in the Application Group selected in 1 in the preceding screenshot.

The VIN VM Dependencies dashboard

This is reached by navigating to **Home** | **Dashboard List** | **VIN** | **VIN VM Dependencies**. The focus of the dashboard is your Virtual Machine list, and it has the following features:

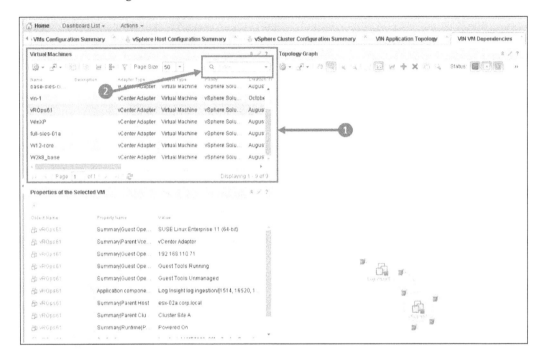

1. The top left panel is a list of all the **Virtual Machines** in your environment. Selecting a Virtual Machine will set the context of:

    ° The **Topology Graph** on the right: This will visualize the applications and dependencies of the selected Virtual Machine

    ° The **Properties** panel below: This is a list of some of the key in-guest properties, such as VMware Tools status, IP address, and the lists of applications and dependencies.

    The dashboard would generally be used when you are troubleshooting or investigating a particular Virtual Machine, and you want to learn more about its applications, and the other Virtual Machines it communicates with, without having to jump into the vSphere Web Client.

2. In a large environment, it is likely the Filter box will be useful to initially narrow down the list of machines.

Summary

In this chapter, we looked at how vRealize Infrastructure Navigator can extend the visibility you have of your vSphere environment.

We first looked at how the solution is deployed, configured, and then integrated into vRealize Operations.

The use, and creation, of Service and Application definitions was examined next, and we looked at both out of the box and custom examples.

Finally, we saw how the solution is integrated with vRealize Operations to give you the visibility you need within a single, central, administrative tool.

In the next chapter, we are going to look at another adjacent administrative tool, vRealize Log Insight.

9
vRealize Log Insight Integration

In this chapter, we are going to look at another of the key adjacencies of vRealize Operations, vRealize Log Insight, and how it can be integrated into vRealize Operations to provide the vSphere administrator with additional troubleshooting capabilities.

The topics that we will cover are as follows:

- Installation of vRealize Log Insight
- Integration with vRealize Operations Manager
- Log Insight Content Packs
- Using agents for operating system and application log monitoring

Introduction to vRealize Log Insight

When you are using vRealize Operations, you are using what can be described as *structured* data.

The solution connects to vSphere, or other infrastructure such as storage, and collects metrics and properties on a regular basis. This **time-series** data is collected at a very consistent cadence, and you are typically collecting values for the same set of metrics and properties each time.

Most system administrators would have been involved in troubleshooting issues where they would have had to dive into logs generated by systems or applications.

Log data is completely different from the data collected by vRealize Operations. It is very *unstructured* data and can be very verbose. There is usually a lot of log data, and finding the information you need is often like "looking for a needle in a haystack."

vRealize Log Insight offers a solution to the problem of **automating** the analysis of this log information. Some of the key capabilities of the solution include the following:

- It can collect logs from a wide variety of sources such as vSphere, Windows and Linux applications, and network and storage devices.

- Logs are structured within the system, which makes it easy for you, as an administrator, to find the information that you need quickly.

- All the logs are in one place; thus, it is easy to correlate logs from, say, vSphere and your network devices when troubleshooting an issue that spans both technology domains.

- The solution is highly scalable — the latest version can ingest up to 180,000 events per second and 2.4 TB of log data per day!

- An ever-increasing number of **Content Packs** are available to provide "out of the box" support for the applications and infrastructure in your environment. For example, Content Packs are available for Microsoft Exchange, SQL, and Active Directory; for network devices from Brocade, Cisco, and Arista; and for storage devices from EMC and Pure Storage.

Installing vRealize Log Insight

One of the really great things about Log Insight is how easy it is to get up and running very quickly. Indeed, within VMware, vRealize Log Insight is considered the "poster child" for ease of installation and use.

As with any software, however, you do still need to carry out a bit of due diligence — read the release notes for the version that you are installing, do some accurate sizing, ensure that you have sufficient computing and storage resources, and ensure that you have the correct network ports opened.

Sizing and design

As mentioned earlier in this chapter, vRealize Log Insight has been designed to support ingestion of up to 180,000 events per second and 2.4 TB of log data per day. For an implementation of this scale, a reasonable amount of design and sizing would, of course, be required.

Let's look at some of the criteria and decision points to consider while sizing and designing your vRealize Log Insight solution.

The solution is, like most VMware products these days, virtual appliance-based, and the appliance can be deployed in four sizes as described in the following extract from the *VMware vRealize Log Insight Getting Started Guide*:

Option	Log Ingest Rate	vCPUs	Memory	IOPS	Syslog Connections	Events per Second
Extra Small	6GB/day	2	4GB	75	20	400
Small	30GB/day	4	8GB	500	100	2000
Medium	75GB/day	8	16GB	1000	250	5000
Large	225GB/day	16	32GB	1500	750	15,000

The different-sized appliances allow you to **scale up** your solution. You may also want to **scale out** your solution by deploying multiple virtual appliances, or nodes, as a cluster. Log Insight supports a cluster with up to 12 nodes. The main reasons to consider clustering are as follows:

- **Scale**: Probably the biggest determining factor. Once you have scaled up to the large appliance, the only way to support more log ingestion will be through scaling out to a multi-node cluster.

- **Availability**: With a multi-node cluster, log ingestion is highly available. If a node goes down, the cluster will still be able to ingest logs.

> For production environments, it is recommended that you use medium or large appliances. This is mainly to provide the required levels of performance when using the solution UI, as opposed to ingestion performance.
>
> Additionally, when deploying as a cluster, a minimum of three nodes are required.

The main criteria for determining the **size** of your appliance node(s) are as follows:

- **Events per Second**: This is the main limiting factor of a node. Once you reach the maximum number of events per second supported by a node, you need to either deploy a larger node or scale out with multiple nodes.

  Every log source will vary in the quantity of events per second that it creates. An ESXi host will typically generate 10 log events per second, so a medium node, which supports 5,000 events per second, can typically support up to 500 ESXi hosts.

- **Event message size**: Log event messages are typically in the range of 150–400 bytes in size. An ESXi log message is typically 170 bytes in size. At a rate of 10 log events per second, this equates to approximately 150 MB per day for each host.

- **Data retention**: How long you intend to keep your logs available for interactive analysis will determine how much storage each node will need. There is a maximum of 4 TB per node, which means that if your data retention period is relatively long, you may need to **scale out** before you hit your ingestion rate limit.

  For example — 500 hosts will generate 75 GB of log data per day. You will consume your 4-TB maximum storage for a single node in approximately 53 days. If you want to retain your data longer than 53 days, you will need to scale out to more data nodes.

  I typically see data retention of 30–60 days. It is not recommended you retain data for longer than 90 days, as any users creating queries for the entire period could cause performance issues.

Thus, once you know how many log sources you will have, an approximation of the messages per second and the size of each message, your required retention period, and whether you want to deploy HA for ingestion, you can do some basic calculations to determine the size and the quantity of nodes that you will require.

One of the experts within the Log Insight community, Steve Flanders, maintains an excellent blog and has written an online sizing calculator that you can use. This is available at `http://sflanders.net/2014/08/20/log-insight-calculator/`.

If you are deploying in a home lab, a single extra-small node will probably suffice!

Appliance installation

Now that you have done the design and sizing, it is time to install and configure vRealize Log Insight.

If you have not yet purchased vRealize Log Insight and want to install an evaluation of the solution, you can download a 60-day evaluation from `http://www.vmware.com/go/try-log-insight`.

Similar to vRealize Operations, the code comes as an OVA file that you install using the vSphere Web Client. To install, follow these steps:

1. In the vSphere Web Client, right-click on the cluster where you want to deploy your vRealize Log Insight node and select **Deploy OVF Template....**

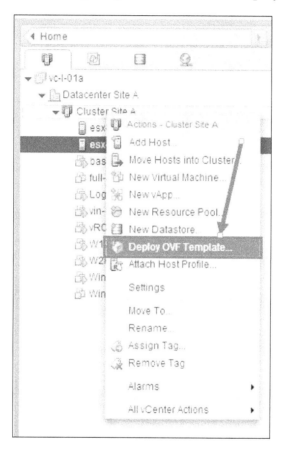

2. Browse to where you have downloaded the OVA installation code and click on **Next** to continue the wizard.

3. Review the OVA details and click on **Next** to continue.

4. Accept the EULA and click on **Next** to continue.

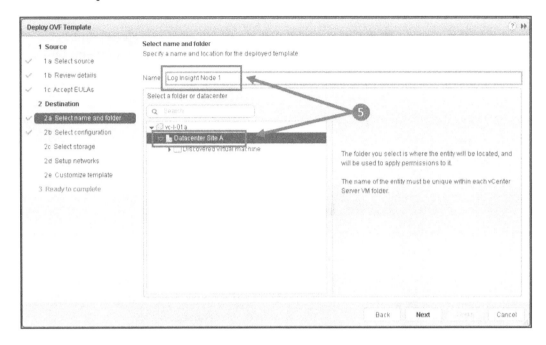

5. Give your appliance a name, for example, **Log Insight Node 1**, select a location to install it and click on **Next** to continue.

6. On the next screen of the wizard, use the drop-down menu to select the node size to install. Click on **Next** to continue.

> Notice the configuration that will be deployed. You will see that the disk size is smaller than what you may ultimately need. Depending on your sizing calculations, you may need to manually resize this later.

7. Select the disk format for your node. For production deployments, the recommendation would be to use Thick Provisioned, Eager Zeroed for best performance.

A vast majority of vRealize Log Insight implementations run with the node(s) storage nearly full in order to maximize the amount of log data available for analysis.

Once the storage reaches 97% used, vRealize Log Insight will automatically delete the oldest logs on a **First in First out** (**FIFO**) basis.

Thus, there is minimal value in implementing with thin provisioning.

8. If you use **storage policies**, you can choose the policy that best meets the IOPS requirements listed in the sizing table.

Do make sure that you choose storage with sufficient IOPS—if you don't, your appliance will not be able to ingest all the logs that are sent to it.

9. Select the **Datastore** on which to install the appliance and click on **Next** to continue.

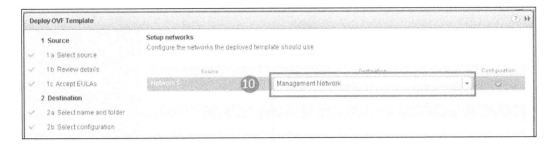

10. Use the dropdown to select the network on which you want to connect your vRealize Log Insight node and click on **Next** to continue. The appliance will need to be on a network that can be reached from all the sources sending logs. It will also need to communicate with your vRealize Operations cluster.

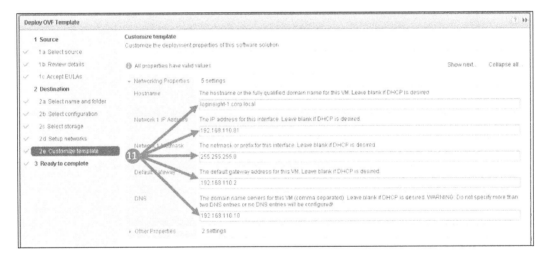

11. On the Customize template page, complete the following:

    ○ **Hostname**: Ensure that you have a forward and reverse DNS record set for your vRealize Log Insight appliance and enter the **FQDN** in this field

    ○ **IP address** for your node

- ° **Netmask**
- ° **Default gateway**
- ° **DNS server(s)**

If you leave the IP address information blank, the appliance will use DHCP when it powers up. I would not recommend this; static IP addressing should be used if possible.

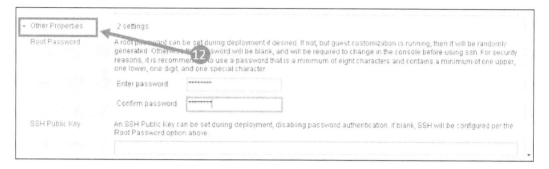

12. Before moving to the next stage in the wizard, click on the arrow to expand the **Other Properties** section. Enter a password for the appliance's **root** account and optionally, enter an **SSH Public Key**. Using an SSH Public Key disables password protection, so the best practice from a security perspective would be to set the root password. Click on **Next** to continue the wizard.

    You can skip this step; however, if you do so, you will need to set the root password in the console later.

13. In the final dialog box, check that you have entered everything correctly; optionally, select the **Power on after deployment** checkbox and click on **Finish** to complete the wizard and deploy the appliance node.

14. The appliance will be installed.

 If you do need to add additional storage, as highlighted in Step 6, now would be a good time to do so. Information on how to do this is documented here: `http://pubs.vmware.com/log-insight-30/index.jsp?topic=%2Fcom.vmware.log-insight.administration.doc%2FGUID-DBC8F35E-369A-4D34-A7AA-96A2C67C9BCC.html`.

```
VMware vRealize Log Insight 3.0.0 Build 3021606


Visit VMware vRealize Log Insight:
http://loginsight-1.corp.local/
http://192.168.110.81/




To access the console, use CTRL+ALT+F1.
    If using a Windows keyboard, press WindowsKey+Alt+F1
    or press Ctrl+Alt+Space, then release the spacebar while
    holding down Ctrl+Alt, and then press F1.
  - If using a Mac keyboard, press Fn+Ctrl+Alt+F1.
  - If the above key combinations do not work, check your keyboard mapping.

To switch back to this screen, use CTRL+ALT+F2.
  - Use the above key combinations but replace F1 with F2.
```

15. Once deployed, you can power up the appliance. On power up, check the appliance's console. When it displays a message similar to that shown in the preceding image, you are ready to start configuring a new vRealize Log Insight deployment.

    If you are installing a multi-node cluster, you should create your additional appliance nodes now. Once all the appliance nodes are built, we can establish the deployment and create the cluster as described next.

Establishing a new deployment

Now that you have installed your appliance node(s), you can establish your vRealize Log Insight deployment with the following steps:

1. Browse to the IP address, or FQDN, of the appliance node that you want as your master node. Ensure that you use a supported browser, as listed in the release notes for the version that you are installing.

2. Click on **Next** to start the wizard.

3. As this is a new deployment, click on **Start New Deployment**.

4. First, you need to set and confirm a password for the built-in admin user. You can optionally set an e-mail address for the admin account. Once done, click on **Save and Continue**.

5. In the next step, enter your license key and again click on **Save and Continue**.

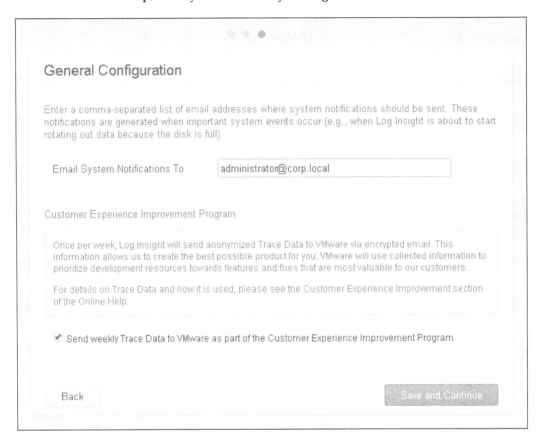

6. In the General Configuration panel, set the following:

    °   An e-mail address where **System Notifications** should be sent.
        You will receive alerts about your deployment at this address—for
        example, if the disk is filling up and logs start rotating out.

   °   Optionally, select the checkbox to have data sent to VMware's Customer Experience Improvement Program. Click on **Save and Continue**.

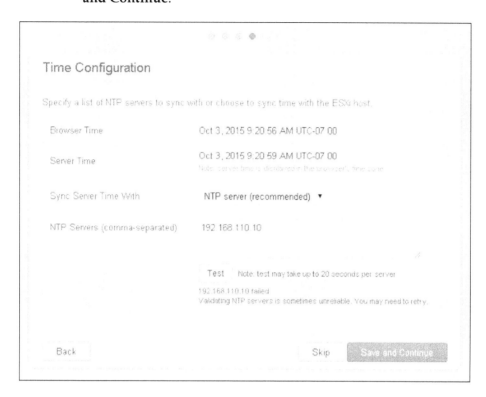

7. Next, configure **Time Synchronization** for your deployment. The recommendation is **Sync Server Time With NTP server**. If you do not have a local NTP server, you can use `pool.ntp.org`. Alternatively, you can sync time with the ESXi host that is hosting your vRealize Log Insight deployment.

Use the **Test** button to check your NTP configuration then select **Save** and **Continue** to continue to the next panel.

8. Now, we need to configure SMTP for outbound e-mail alerting. Set the following parameters:

   ° **SMTP**: Name of your SMTP host receiving e-mails

   ° **Port**: SMTP port used by this host

   ° **SSL (SMTPS)**: Whether SSL is required

   ° **STARTTLS Encryption**: Whether STARTTLS encryption is enabled on the host

   ° **Sender**: This will populate the "From" field in the e-mails that will be sent

   ° **Username** and **Password**: Fill these fields in if your SMTP server requires them

   Click on **Save and Continue** to continue to the last panel.

9. Finally, click on **Finish** to complete the **initial configuration**.

This completes the initial configuration of your vRealize Log Insight deployment. The solution is now ready to ingest data as shown by the splash screen that you will now see.

At this point, you can add further nodes to your cluster if required. The following section describes how to do this. If you are only deploying a single node, you can skip forward to the Log Ingestion section of this chapter.

Adding nodes to the cluster

You don't need to immediately add nodes to your cluster. However, as soon as you start configuring your log sources to send logs to your vRealize Log Insight deployment, the load on the system will, of course, increase.

It may, therefore, make sense to add the required additional nodes to the cluster before you start configuring the log sources for ingestion. The following steps describe how to add nodes to your cluster.

1. Browse to the IP address, or FQDN, of the appliance node that you want to add as a data node.

2. Click on **Next** at the welcome screen.

3. Click on **Join an Existing Deployment**.

4. In the **Join an Existing Deployment** dialog box, enter the FQDN of the master vRealize Log Insight node and click on **Go**.

5. To complete the installation, you will need to navigate to the **Cluster Management** page of your master node. Click on the **Cluster Management** link then click on **Allow** to add the node as a worker.

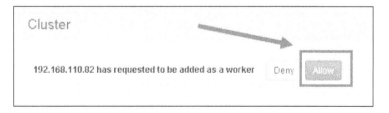

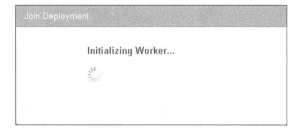

6. The Worker node being added will take a few minutes to initialize. You can go back to its browser tab to monitor progress. Once complete, click on **OK** to finish.

Complete the above steps until you have installed all the nodes required for your cluster. The minimum number of nodes required is 3.

Configuring Integrated Load Balancer

The final step when configuring a cluster is to configure an IP address and FQDN for **Integrated Load Balancer (ILB)**.

 Before configuring the ILB, ensure that you have configured appropriate forward **and** reverse DBS records for it.

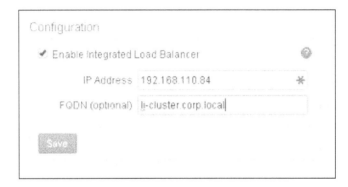

On the Cluster Administration page, select the **Enable Integrated Load Balancer** checkbox and enter the **IP address** and **FQDN** that will act as the load balancer.

Click on **Save** to continue.

 Note: For the rest of this chapter, if you have deployed a cluster, when IP Addresses or FQDNs of the vRealize Log Insight instance are referred to, use the IP address or FQDN of the ILB.

Log ingestion

Now that your vRealize Log Insight platform is established, you can start sending logs to the platform. There are three main methods to do so:

- **vSphere Integration**: vCenters and Hosts send all their logs

- **Agents**: Agents are installed on Windows and Linux to send files or event logs

- **Syslog**: Any device running Syslog can add vRealize Log Insight as a Syslog destination

Logging in

To access vRealize Log Insight, enter the *IP Address* or *FQDN* of your vRealize Log Insight instance into your browser and accept the self-signed certificate if required. The login screen will appear — for now, only the Admin account is configured so use that along with the password that you set in the *Establishing a new Deployment* section earlier.

As no systems have yet been configured to send logs, the following wizard will show when you log into vRealize Log Insight for the first time.

vSphere integration and log ingestion

The first thing most administrators will configure is integration with vSphere to collect logs from ESXi hosts and vCenters.

Out of the box, this is very easy to configure. Click on the **Configure vSphere** integration link in the wizard shown in the preceding screenshot. This will bring up a panel that can be configured as follows:

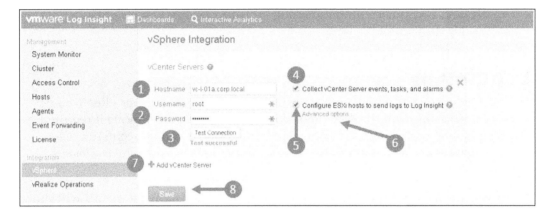

1. Enter the **Hostname** for the first vCenter that you want to collect logs from.

2. Enter a **Username** and **Password** with sufficient permissions on the vCenter server. The required permissions are as follows:

   ° To collect Events, Tasks, and Alarms from vCenter, *System.View* is required. This privilege can be provided by the *Read Only* role.

   ° To additionally allow vRealize Log Insight to perform reconfiguration of Syslog on your ESXi hosts, the *Host.Configuration. Change* and *Host.Configuration.Network* permissions are required.

3. Check your credentials by using the **Test Connection** button.

4. Select the checkbox to allow the collection of vCenter Events, Tasks, and Alarms.

5. Select the checkbox to have your ESXi hosts automatically configured to send logs to your vRealize Log Insight deployment.

 This configuration won't overwrite any Syslog configuration that you already have set on your ESXi hosts. It will simply add your vRealize Log Insight deployment as a destination for log events.

6. You can click on **Advanced Options** to select specific hosts that you may, or may not, want to configure to send logs to your vRealize Log Insight deployment. You would most probably do this in a large environment as you may not wish to reconfigure all your ESXi hosts at once.

7. If you have more than one vCenter, click on the *plus* icon, to open a panel to allow you to configure connectivity to your additional vCenter(s).

   The solution supports connection to up to 10 vCenters.

8. Finally, click on **Save** to complete your configuration.

With just a few clicks and entries, your entire vSphere estate has been configured to send all its logs to vRealize Log Insight. These logs will immediately be ingested and analyzed. We will look at how you can use this log data later in this chapter.

Syslog ingestion

Out of the box, vRealize Log Insight is a **Syslog** server and can, therefore, consume logs from other devices that use Syslog.

The default Syslog ports of *514/TCP, 1514/TCP,* and *514/UDP* are used.

To use this capability, you simply have to configure hosts and devices to send their logs to your vRealize Log Insight instance.

In the preceding section, all of our ESXi hosts would have been configured to do this automatically. Let's have a look at how these hosts have been configured, and how we could manually configure them if necessary.

You can use the vSphere Web Client to review the configuration as follows:

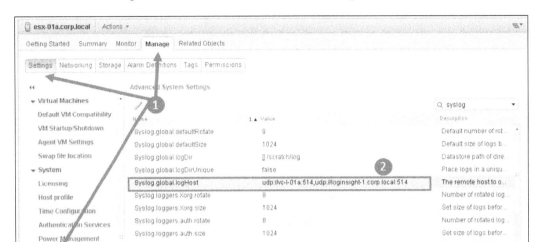

1. Navigate to one of your hosts in the vSphere Web Client, and select **Manage | Settings | Advanced System Settings**.

2. Scroll down to **Syslog.global.logHost**, and you will notice that your vRealize Log Insight has been added to the list of hosts using the **udp://LogInsightHostFQDN:514** format.

Collection agents

As well as ingesting logs from vCenter, your ESXi hosts, and any other device with Syslog, you can use Windows and Linux **Collection Agents** to send logs that aren't readily available through Syslog.

To get started with this, you will need to navigate, within vRealize Log Insight, to the Administration screen:

1. Click on the *drop-down menu* icon in the top right-hand corner of the vRealize Log Insight UI.

2. Select **Administration**.

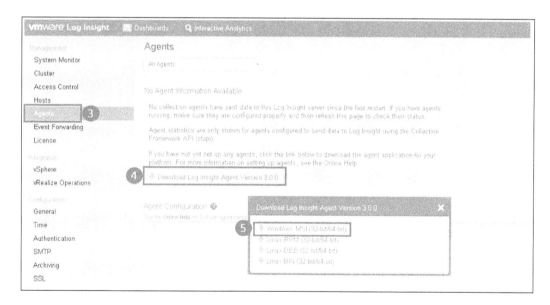

3. Now, select **Agents** from the left-hand menu.

4. Click on **Download Log Insight Agent** to open up the download dialog box.

5. Here, you can download **Windows** and **Linux** agents. For this exercise, we are going to download the **Windows** agent and install it on our AD server. Clicking on the link will download the MSI installable agent.

Installing the Windows agent

The Windows agent comes as a standard MSI installer for 32-bit or 64-bit Windows. The process to install is as follows:

1. Double-click on the `.msi` file to start the installation.

2. Accept the license and click on **Next** to continue.

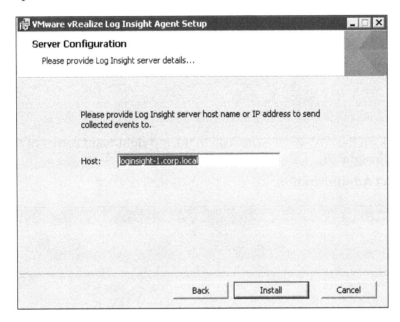

3. Host should be auto-populated with the FQDN of your vRealize Log Insight host. Click on **Install** to complete the agent installation.

4. If you go back to vRealize Log Insight and refresh your browser, you should now see in **Administration | Agents** that your agent has successfully registered. You will also notice that it hasn't yet sent any events. This is because we have not configured it yet—you will see that the Agent Configuration section at the bottom is blank.

Agent groups and agent configuration

The Windows and Linux agents that you install will not send any log messages to vRealize Log Insight until you configure them to do so. In essence, you have to tell the agents where to look for logs and messages, and their format.

You can do this in the following two ways:

- **Client side**: You modify the settings file on each individual agent. This can become unwieldy as you scale the number of agents deployed.

- **Server side**: You configure your vRealize Log Insight deployment with settings for your agents. This used to be relatively inflexible, as you were generally limited to a single configuration for all your agents.

  With the launch of Version 3.0 of vRealize Log Insight, however, **Agent Groups** were introduced, which has made server side configuration much more flexible.

With these new Agent Groups available, you should, therefore, generally adopt server side configuration for your agents.

One of the other useful new features in Version 3.0 is the integration of Agent Groups with Content Packs. This makes configuring these new Agent Groups a very simple exercise.

So, let's first explore Content Packs, and then, we will go on and configure the Agent Groups to support the Windows agent that we have installed.

Content Packs

The most valuable part of vRealize Log Insight is **Content**, and this is provided by way of **Content Packs**.

Without these Content Packs, the solution would simply be a Log Aggregator with a very useful, high-performing, and intuitive UI. Content Packs add the much needed intellectual property around the applications and devices that they represent.

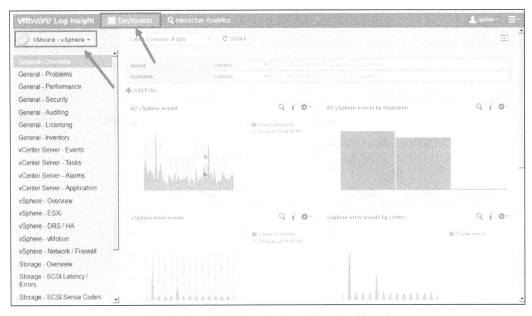

vRealize Log Insight showing the vSphere Dashboard

Out of the box, the **vSphere Content Pack** is included, and if you navigate to Dashboards, you will see the **VMware – vSphere** dashboards created by this Content Pack.

Adding additional Content Packs

To add Content Packs, you first need to navigate to the **Content Pack** marketplace.

1. Click on the **Menu** icon on the top right-hand corner of the UI.
2. Select **Content Packs**. This will take you to the **Content Pack Marketplace**.

Here, you will see all the Content Packs that have been written for vRealize Log Insight. You can install as many Content Packs as you like, and there is no additional charge for them.

For now, we'll add the following Content Packs:

- **Microsoft – Windows**
- **Microsoft – Active Directory**
- **VMware – vR Ops 6.x**

Click on the icon for each Content Pack in turn and select **Install**.

This will install the Content Pack and open a dialog box with any specific installation instructions required for that Content Pack.

For example, the Microsoft Windows content pack describes how you need to reconfigure your Windows system if you want to take advantage of some of the Audit dashboard capabilities.

Review the details and click on **OK** to close the dialog box for each Content Pack.

Viewing installed Content Packs

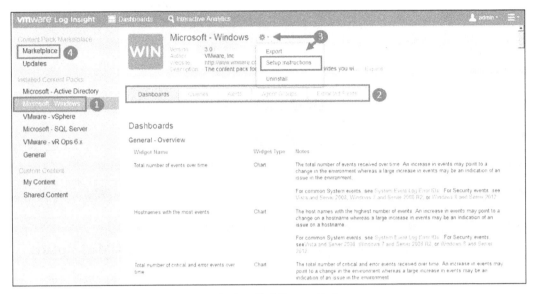

Viewing installed Content Packs

Once installed, your Content Packs will be listed in the left-hand menu in Content Packs, as shown in the preceding screenshot.

1. Click on the **Content Pack** that you want to view on the left-hand menu.

2. There are several tabs available to describe the Content Pack:

    ° **Dashboards**: A list of the dashboards that the Content Pack creates, with a description for each and some detail on what it shows.

    ° **Queries**: Standalone queries that are available within the dashboards. When executed, these will open the **Interactive Analysis** UI in context.

    ° **Alerts**: A list of alerts that can be enabled and are specific to this Content Pack.

    ° **Agent groups**: The Agent Groups that are created by the Content Pack and the agent settings that are applied by these Agent Groups.

    ° **Extracted Fields**: The fields that are defined by the Content Pack, which are extracted for use by dashboards and within Interactive Analysis.

3. Clicking on the cog icon allows you to review the **Setup instructions** that are displayed when the Content Pack is installed. This is also where you would un-install the Content Pack.

4. After you have installed the Content Pack, you can navigate back to the Content Pack marketplace by clicking on **Marketplace** in the left-hand menu.

Using Content Pack Agent Groups

Now that you have installed your Content Packs, you can go ahead and make use of the Templates that have been installed and create some Agent Groups.

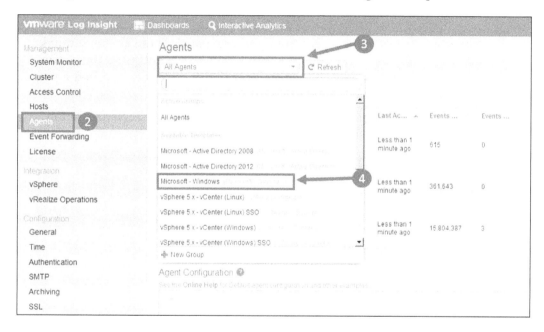

1. Click on the **Menu** icon in the top right hand corner of the UI and select **Administration**.

2. Click on **Agents** to view your list of agents.

3. Select the **All Agents** dropdown to open the list of available **Groups** and **Templates** that can be applied to your Collection Agents.

4. Click on **Microsoft – Windows** to select this first template.

5. Notice the details in the Agent Configuration panel. These are the settings that will configure your Windows agents to collect events from the various Windows Event Log Channels. You can edit this section as required if you wish to include or exclude specific channels.

   Click on **Copy Template** to copy these settings for the next configuration step.

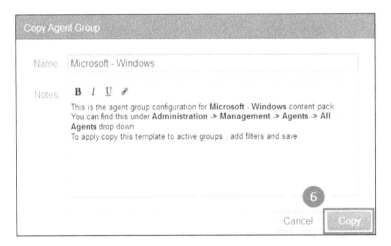

6. You can change the name of the Agent Group and add details of any changes you may have made from the defaults, as shown in the preceding dialog box. Once complete, click on **Copy** to proceed to the final configuration step.

Agent Group filters and configuration review

7. The final step is to create some **filters** for this Agent Group. When you create filters, you have the option to filter on the basis of the following:
    ° IP address
    ° Hostname
    ° Version
    ° OS

In this case, we should select **OS** and have the criteria **starts with** and a value of **Microsoft Windows**.

8. You can review the settings that will be applied in the Agent Configuration box.

9. Finally, click on **Save New Group** to save your Agent Group.

   This Agent Group will now be **dynamic**. Any new agents pointing to this instance of vRealize Log Insight will have these settings applied if their operating system is Microsoft Windows.

   Agent Groups should be created for each Content Pack that you install — this will complete configuration of the agents on your managed devices.

Manual configuration

Content Packs usually contain everything that you need for installation and configuration and are generally easy to navigate.

Unfortunately, this is not the case for all Content Packs. In some cases, you have to do some manual configuration. An example of this is the **vR Ops 6.1** Content Pack that we installed earlier.

If you look at the Content Pack description for this Content Pack, you will see the following notification:

> **IMPORTANT:** The Log Insight agent uses the cfapi and specific tags are required for this content pack to work. For directions on proper agent configuration see the Solution Exchange listing.

Some Content Packs, as shown in the above dialogue box, will refer you to Solution Exchange, where you may need to download detailed installation documentation.

 As discussed in *Chapter 7, vRealize Operations Manager Solutions* VMware's Solution Exchange is available at `http://solutionexchange.vmware.com`.

Configuring vRealize Operations Management Content Pack

As described above, some of the content packs require some manual configuration of the Log Insight agent. Let's take a high-level look at the steps required to configure the vRealize Operations Content Pack.

To complete these steps, you will need to enable SSH and create a Root password on your vRealize Operations cluster nodes. Information on how to do this is provided in the following VMware Knowledge Base article: `http://kb.vmware.com/selfservice/microsites/search.do?language=en_US&cmd=displayKC&externalId=2100515`

The vRealize Log Insight Linux agent is pre-installed on installations of vRealize Operations v6.02 or later; therefore, we only need to configure it:

1. Using a text editor, such as VI or the text editing functionality in WinSCP, you need to edit **/VAR/LIB/LOGINSIGHT-AGENT/liagent.ini** on each vRealize Operations node and provide the address of your vRealize Log Insight instance. You need the following three lines:

   ```
   hostname=IPAddressorFQDNofYourLogInsightNodeorILB
   proto=cfapi
   port=9000
   ```

2. The agent now needs to be configured to look for the 19 different log sources on your vRealize Operations nodes, as described, and using the code in the installation documentation at `https://solutionexchange.vmware.com/store/products/vrealize-operations-manager-content-pack-for-log-insight/files/21977`.

   You can either copy the example code from the installation documentation into the `liagent.ini` file on each vRealize Operations cluster node or create a new Agent Group as described earlier in this chapter.

   You will need to manually update some of the tags in the example code to reflect your environment. For example, `vmw_vr_ops_hostname` should be changed to the IP address or FQDN of your vRealize Operations Manager node.

   You will need to complete the agent configuration on each of your vRealize Operations Manager nodes. The use of Agent Groups will therefore be the easiest way to accomplish this.

vRealize Operations Manager integration

vRealize Log Insight integrates with vRealize Operations Manager to deliver two key areas of additional functionality:

- **Log Data Alerts**: Alerts from vRealize Log Insight can be forwarded as events to vRealize Operations in order to provide additional troubleshooting capability.

- **Launch in Context**: When troubleshooting an object in vRealize Operations, an additional menu item is provided in the dashboards to launch vRealize Log Insight in context. If selected, this will navigate the administrator directly to the Interactive Analysis screen in vRealize Log Insight for that object. This will enable further troubleshooting using the unstructured log events in vRealize Log Insight.

Configuring the integration requires you to follow two steps in the following order:

1. Install the vRealize Log Insight Management Pack.
2. Configure the integration in vRealize Log Insight.

Installing the Log Insight Management Pack in vRealize Operations

As with all Management Packs, the Management Pack for vRealize Log Insight is downloadable from VMware's Solution Exchange website.

Once downloaded, we can install this in the same way as we installed the NSX Management Pack in *Chapter 7, vRealize Operations Manager Solutions*. The only difference is that no additional configuration is required for this Management Pack.

Configuring the integration in vRealize Log Insight

Once the Management Pack is installed, the final step is to configure the integration in vRealize Log Insight as follows:

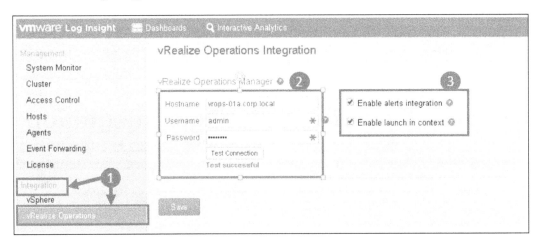

1. In the vRealize Log Insight UI, navigate to **Administration | Integration | vRealize Operations**.

2. Enter the **FQDN**, **Username**, and **Password** for your vRealize Operations instance. Click on **Test Connection** to ensure that the details are entered correctly.

3. Select the checkboxes for the following:

    ○   **Enable alerts integration**: This allows alerts within vRealize Log Insight to be sent to vRealize Operations and acted upon within that platform

    ○   **Enable launch in context**: This adds an item to the **Actions** menu in vRealize Operations that allows you to launch vRealize Log Insight in context from a VM's or host's dashboard

Using vRealize Log Insight with vRealize Operations Manager

Now that we have installed and configured vRealize Log Insight, we'll take a look at how the integrations with vRealize Operations Manager are surfaced.

Orientation

We won't seek to cover "How to use" vRealize Log Insight here, as that would probably be a book in its own right! We will, however, provide an orientation of the UI in this section.

The following are the three main areas of the UI that you will be using:

*   **Dashboards**: Content Packs will typically install a number of vRealize Log Insight dashboards to help visualize the log events flowing into the solution.

    For example, the vSphere Content Pack comes with 23 dashboards, covering everything from performance, security, vCenter tasks and alerts, vMotions, and networking to storage, and much more!

*   **Interactive analysis**: You will use interactive analysis when you drill down into a subject and look at the logs in more detail or further refine your queries.

*   **Administration**: We have already used administration to configure the solution and add Content Packs.

Dashboards

Let's take a look at the **Dashboards** view.

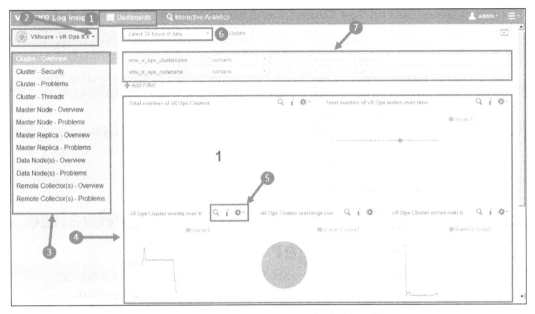

The anatomy of vRealize Log Insight dashboards

1. You can always navigate back to dashboards by clicking on the **Dashboards** link.

2. In the top-left corner, you select the Content Pack that you wish to view using this dropdown. In this case, we are looking at the **VMware – vR Ops 6.x** Content Pack.

3. Below the Content Packs selector is the list of **Dashboards** for that Content Pack.

4. Dashboards are made up of one or more **Widgets**, which are displayed in the main panel.

5. The widget action buttons allow you to do the following:

    ○   Enter **Interactive Analysis** in the widget's context.

    ○   Display **information** about the widget and the content that it shows.

    ○   **Clone** the widget—this allows you to create a new widget by using the current widget configuration as your starting point.

6. **Time period**: Here, you select the time period of logs that your dashboard will show.

7. **Filters**: Most dashboards will have filters, so you can zero-in on a more refined context without having to navigate to **Interactive Analysis**. For example, you may be interested in the dashboard representing just a subset of your hosts.

Interactive analysis

The **Interactive Analysis** screen is used as follows:

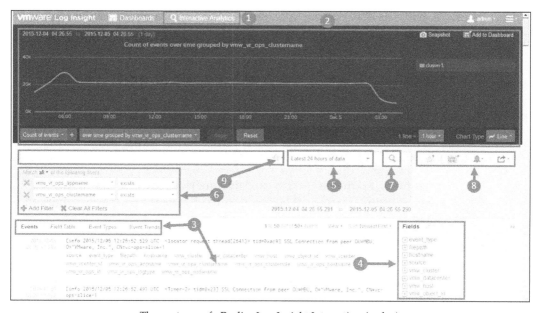

The anatomy of vRealize Log Insight Interactive Analysis

1. Navigate to Interactive Analysis by using the link at the top of the UI.

2. You can create a visualization of the query — there are many options to control the look of this visualization by using the button controls.

3. The log events themselves are displayed in the main panel. There are four tabs to control what this panel displays:

    ° **Events**: These are the raw log entries. The extracted fields are linkable and colored blue.

    ° **Field Table**: The extracted fields displayed as a table showing the log events sortable by field.

- **Event Type**: This tab groups all the events of each **Event Type** together, listing them in the order of Event Type with the most events. This allows you to see the most common Event Types being logged.

- **Event Trends**: This is a new feature in version 3.0 of vRealize Log Insight. It is similar to the Event Type tab but looks at the trend of the number of each Event Type. This allows you to see the events that are starting to be logged on a more regular basis.

4. **Fields**: This is a list of the fields defined by Content Packs or Log Insight that are extracted and indexed. You can extract fields yourself if there is text or numeric patterns that you are specifically looking for within a set of logs.

5. **Time period**: Here, you select the time period of logs that your dashboard will show.

6. The context of interactive analysis is set by **filters**. You can add/remove/change all these filters in this panel.

7. **Search**: This searches the log dataset after you make changes to the other sections in the UI. It is also used if you want to refresh the data or panels.

8. **Action Buttons**: There are four buttons that allow you to do the following:

   - **Set favorite queries** — You can save queries that you commonly use as **Favorites**. These will be listed in the **Favorites** dropdown marked **9** in the preceding screenshot.

   - **Add current query to dashboard** — This creates a widget representing the current query in either an existing or a new dashboard.

   - **Create or manage alerts** — This allows you to create an alert out of the query. We will look at this in the next section of this chapter.

   - **Export or share current query** — You can export the results of the query or chart as raw data, CSV, or JSON. The query can also be shared with another vRealize Log Insight user via a custom URL that will be generated.

Creating alerts to be sent to vRealize Operations Manager

Using vRealize Log Insight, you can create notification events in vRealize Operations Manager. Let's run through a simple scenario to help describe how this works.

Scenario

The vSphere Content Pack has a widget that reports on log events, describing console commands executed on your ESXi hosts.

We would like to be notified and be able to see in vRealize Operations when specific console commands have been executed on a particular host.

Creating alert

As can be seen in the following screenshot, the **General – Security** dashboard in the vSphere Content Pack has a widget that displays the ESXi shell commands that have been executed on all the monitored hosts. We can see that the reboot command has been executed!

Clicking on the *Interactive Analysis* icon will allow us to look at this in more detail and create an **Alert**.

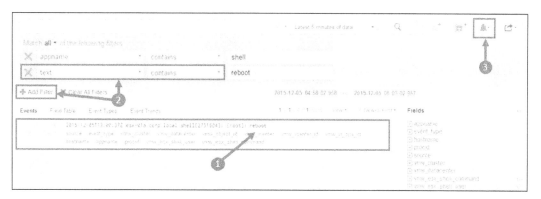

Creating an Alert

1. We can see the filtered log events in the main pane.

2. Rather than be sent an alert for every command sent to ESXi, we would like to filter the list of log events further. To do this, click on the **Add Filter** button; and in this case, I have added a filter to look for the following text: **reboot**.

3. To create the alert, click on the **Alert** icon and select **Create Alert** from the query.

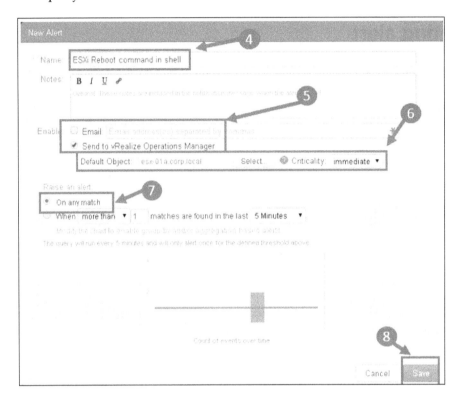

4. Give the alert a **name**: It's useful to be quite verbose here, as this name will become part of the notification alert in vRealize Operations.

5. Select the **Send to vRealize Operations Manager** checkbox—you can optionally send an **e-mail alert** as well.

6. Now, choose the **Object** on which to alert. In this case, I have selected the **esx-01a.corp.lcoal** host and have set the **criticality** of the alert to **immediate**. This will set the criticality of the alert within vRealize Operations.

7. In this case, I want to raise the alert when **any** event comes through with a **reboot** shell command. In some cases, you may be creating alerts when you see specific **quantities** of an event.

8. Finally, click on **Save** to create and activate the **Alert**.

Viewing alerts in vRealize Operations

Now, if we look at the **Alerts Dashboard** in vRealize Operations, we can see that the alert has flowed through, as can be seen in the following screenshot:

With the alert flowing through, we can, if desired, leverage recommendations and actions within the alerting framework to add a further operational workflow to the alert symptoms identified.

Launching in context from vRealize Operations Manager

Launching in context is simple!

In the following screenshot, I have clicked through to the dashboard for the host with the reboot alert that we just created. You would use this when, for example, you see an alert or badge degradation in vRealize Operations and need to drill down into the logs of the monitored object for more details.

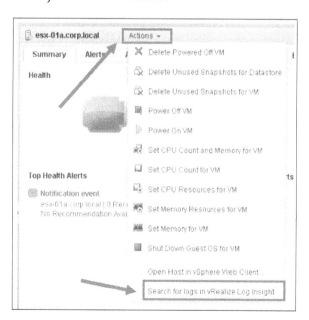

Click on **Actions** and then **Search for logs in vRealize Log Insight...** to launch vRealize Log Insight in the context of that host.

Summary

In this chapter, we have looked at the integration of one of the key adjacencies to vRealize Operations, Log Insight.

We have discussed how to install and configure the solution, how to extend it with Content Packs and Agents, and how the solution integrates with vRealize Operations.

In the next chapter, we will look at a further extension of vRealize Operations, End Point Operations Management.

10
End Point Operations

In the previous chapter, we looked at how you can extend vRealize Operations by adding the troubleshooting capabilities of vRealize Log Insight. This included capturing logs, not just from vSphere but also from operating systems and applications.

In this last chapter, we will look at how you can monitor your operating systems and applications further with the addition of End Point Operations. The topics that we will cover are as follows:

- End Point Operations history and architecture
- Deploying End Point Operations
- Content within End Point Operations
- Adapting policies to meet monitoring requirements

Introduction to End Point Operations

End Point Operations was introduced with the release of vRealize Operations 6.1. It's not, however, a brand new capability; it's more of an evolution of an existing technology.

Prior to the availability of End Point Operations, the solution used for managing in guest operating systems and applications was **vRealize Hyperic**. The vRealize Hyperic solution consists of the following:

- One or more Hyperic HQ servers
- In-guest agent to collect metrics and properties and send them to Hyperic HQ
- The Hyperic Management Pack in vRealize Operations to collect data from Hyperic HQ

With vRealize Operations, the Hyperic HQ servers are no longer required—the agents, now renamed **End Point Operations agents**, send the operating system and application metrics and properties directly to vRealize Operations.

The move of vRealize Hyperic into vRealize Operations is not yet complete, so you can still deploy vRealize Hyperic; however, if End Point Operations meets your needs, then it is the way to go in order to provide guest monitoring and troubleshooting.

Over time, it is expected that End Point Operations will completely replace Hyperic within the vRealize Operations solution.

Licensing

End Point Operations licensing is provided as part of your vRealize Operations Manager license. There are two editions that enable the End Point Operations functionality:

- **vRealize Operations Advanced**: This allows you to monitor and manage operating systems
- **vRealize Operations Enterprise**: This allows you to monitor and manage applications

Deploying End Point Operations

The End Point Operations **Agents** are available from My VMware in the same place as the main vRealize Operations Manager downloads at `https://my.vmware.com/group/vmware/details?downloadGroup=VROPS-610&productId=538&rPId=9050`.

 You will only see the End Point Operations downloads if you are entitled to the Advanced or Enterprise editions of vRealize Operations.

You will see quite a number of downloads; to choose the correct one, you need to consider the following:

- **Windows or Linux**: Agents are available for both. The release notes will confirm the exact versions of these operating systems that are supported.
- **Java Runtime Engine (JRE)**: There are agents available that ship with, or without a JRE. An agent without the JRE is slightly lighter in weight; however, you will need to make sure that you have a supported JRE, as described in the release notes. This also means that you need to be careful when you update your JRE.

For this reason, I tend to use the agent that comes with its own JRE.

- **32-bit or 64-bit**: Choose the version that matches the guest OS you are installing the software on.

- `zip` or `.exe`, `tar` or `.rpm`: For a one-time installation, just the `.exe` or `.rpm` format is the easiest. If you want to modify the setup parameters, for example, the `agent.properties` file, then use the `.zip` or `.tar` format.

Deploying the Windows agent

Let's step through how you can install the End Point Operations agent on your Windows systems. We'll use the `.exe` installation media in this case:

1. Double-click on the appropriate `.exe` file (32-bit or 64-bit) to start the installation, and click on **Next** to continue.

2. Enter the **FQDN** of your vRealize Operations server and leave the **Secure Port** setting at the default of **443**; click on **Next** to continue.

3. Next, you need the Certificate **thumbprint** of your vRealize Operations cluster.

   At this stage, the installation wizard points you at the documentation for more information. Unfortunately, it is not particularly clear in the documentation, so here is some detail on where to get your thumbprint!

4. Navigate to the **Admin URL** of your vRealize Operations instance. This will be `http://FQDNorIPAddress/admin` and log in using the admin credentials that you set during the installation of vRealize Operations.

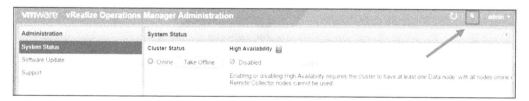

5. Next, click on the *certificate* icon on the top right-hand corner to view the certificates in place.

6. You will see two certificate thumbprints. You need to make a note of, or copy, the **second** one on the list — this is the one related to your vRealize Operations Cluster.

7. Paste this thumbprint into the dialogue box in your End Point Operations Wizard, and click on **Next** to continue.

8. Now, you need to enter administrative credentials for your vRealize Operations instance.

9. Accept the EULA, and click on **Next** to continue.

10. Either accept the default, or change the location of the folder where you would like the End Point Operations agent installed. Click on **Next** to continue.

11. The End Point Operations agent will now complete installation. Once installed, you should start to see objects appear in vRealize Operations.

Viewing your End Points in vRealize Operations

One of the really useful things with vRealize Operations is how it creates relationships between your virtual machine objects and the new operating system objects.

To take a look at this, in vRealize Operations, navigate to a virtual machine on which you have an End Point Operations agent installed. Select the **Troubleshooting | All Metrics** dashboard, and you will see the relationship tree, as in the following screenshot.

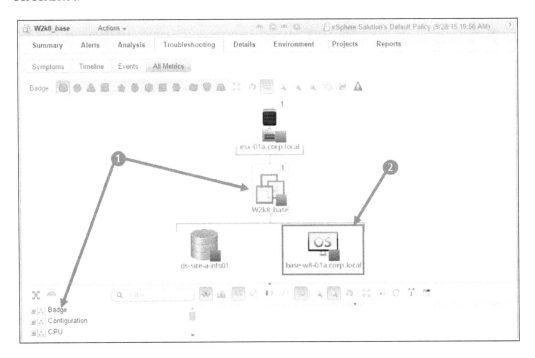

1. Notice the lightly dashed red box around the selected Virtual Machine object. This means everything else in the view is in the context of this object.

   For example, the metric selector will allow the selection of metrics for this object to be displayed in the metrics panel.

2. The End Point Operations object appears as a *child* of the Virtual Machine.

3. Clicking on this object would change the view's context—you would see the operating system metrics in the metric selector. This would allow you to see metric graphs of both the Virtual Machine and the operating system side by side.

The End Point Operations objects become first-class citizens within vRealize Operations and can be viewed in various different dashboards and contexts.

If you wanted to, for example, get a view of your entire Windows estate, you could navigate to **Environment Overview | Inventory Trees | Operating Systems**.

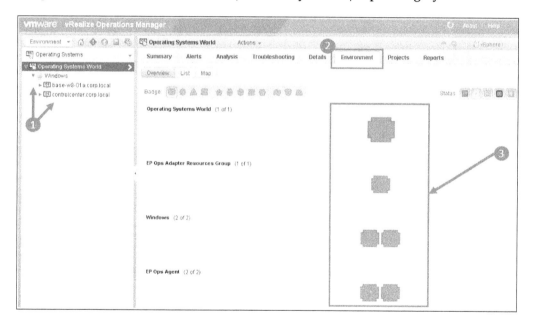

1. Click on **Operating Systems World**, and expand the hierarchy to see the operating systems and the agents installed on each operating system.

2. Click on the **Environment** tab of **Operating Systems World** to get a view of all the objects.

3. Here, you can see the hierarchical view of all your operating system objects.

Service monitoring in Windows

Along with the core competency of collecting, monitoring, and alerting on metrics and properties, with the End Point Operation agent, we can look further into the operating systems and monitor **Services**.

For example, you may want to monitor the uptime or usage of a Windows service, and report or alert on it within vRealize Operations. To achieve this, do the following:

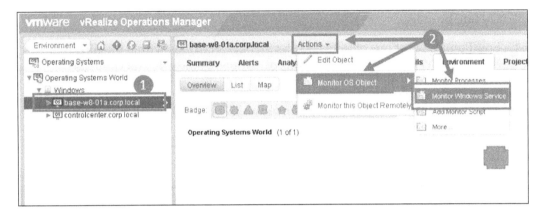

1. Select the **Operating System** object on which you want to monitor a particular Windows Service.

2. Click on the **Actions** menu, and select **Monitor OS Object | Monitor Windows Service**.

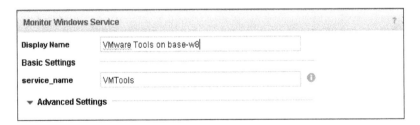

3. In the **Monitor Windows Service** panel, enter the following information:

    ○   **Display Name**: Along with naming the service that you are monitoring, it may be worth including the host's name. This is because this monitored service will become an object within vRealize Operations in its own right.

○ **service_name**: Name of the **Windows Service**. You can find this name in the Windows Service panel within Windows.

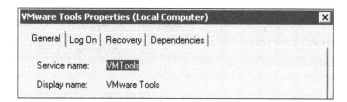

For example, the **VMware Tools** service is called **VMTools**, as shown in the preceding screenshot.

4. Click on **OK** to save the Windows Service definition.

Now, when we look at our virtual machine within **Troubleshooting | All Metrics**, we can see a richer hierarchy:

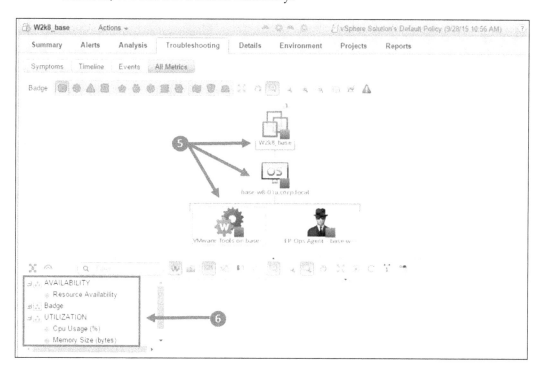

5. The virtual machine is a **parent** of the operating system, which is a **parent** of the newly defined VMware Tools service.

6. Clicking on the **VMware Tools** service brings up its metric selector. We can see the following:

   ° A metric called **Resource Availability**: This will allow us to monitor, alert, and report on the availability or uptime of this service.

   ° **UTILIZATION**: These are metrics showing the CPU and memory utilization of the service.

> In the **Utilization** section, you will see that there are only two metrics passed to vRealize Operations by the service. There are an additional 11 metrics available to you. You can enable these in the **5. Collect Metrics and Properties** section of the policy applied to the Service object. We will look at this in more detail later in this chapter.
>
> A screenshot of the metrics disabled as default is as follows:

Along with monitoring services, you can select **Actions | Monitor OS Object | Monitor Processes** to monitor individual Windows **Processes**.

In addition to this, other monitoring objects such as remote monitoring of the website availability or the server availability via **ICMP** can be created within the End Point Operations framework.

End Point Operations Solution Packs

So far, we have looked at the monitoring of just an operating system—in the preceding examples, the Windows operating system.

The End Point Operations framework has been built to monitor **applications** as well as operating systems.

When you deploy End Point Operations agents, unlike vRealize Hyperic, the agents do not automatically understand and manage every supported application. The core agent is now designed only to initially understand the most common end points, such as the Microsoft Windows operating system.

As described in *Chapter 7, vRealize Operations Manager Solutions*, a lot of the additional End Point Operations content is provided via Solution Packs in VMware Solution Exchange. You can expect an ever-increasing range of supported applications to be made available in Solutions Exchange.

Implementing Solution Packs

In this section, we will go through the implementation and configuration of a Solution Pack. In this case, we will look at *Microsoft SQL Solution for vRealize Operations*.

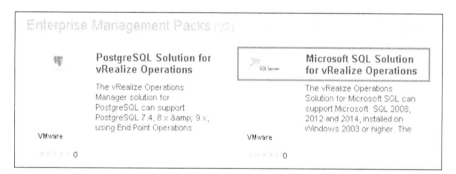

The first step is to locate the Solution Pack on VMware's Solution Exchange and download it.

As with everything that you download from Solutions Exchange, you should always check the release notes and installation instructions.

Although the installation of most of the content on Solutions Exchange can be considered generic, there will often be specific requirements, or subtleties, that are called out in the documentation.

The Microsoft SQL solution for vRealize Operations requires a minor change in the End Point Operations agent. The agent will need to be configured as a *domain user*, unless you are running a Microsoft SQL server not integrated with Active Directory.

This is quite a straightforward task:

1. On the server being monitored, open Services and look for the **End Point Operations Management Agent** service.
2. Double-click on the service to open it, and select the **Log On** tab.
3. Select the log on as **This account** as the credentials for the End Point Operations agent to use.
4. Restart the End Point agent service to apply the change.

Now, we can go ahead and install the solution within vRealize Operations Manager.

1. Navigate to **Administration | Solutions**, and click on the *Plus* icon to start.

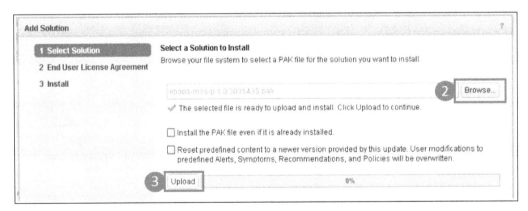

2. Click on **Browse** to locate the **PAK file** that you downloaded from Solution Exchange.

3. Click on **Upload** to start the installation.

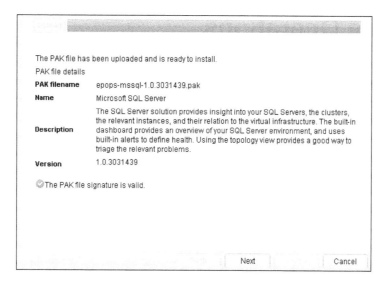

4. Once the PAK file is ready for installation, click on **Next** to continue.
5. Accept the EULA, and click on **Next** to continue.
6. Once installed, click on **Finish** to complete the installation wizard.

Once the Solution Pack is installed, a number of things will happen:

*   The **MS SQL Dashboard** will be created in the **Dashboards | Applications** folder.
*   Some **Alert, Symptoms**, and **Recommendations** will be created specifically for Microsoft SQL Server.
*   The **Microsoft SQL Server Plug-in** will be installed in **Administration | Plug-ins**.
*   Any End Point Operations agents on hosts running Microsoft SQL will have the Microsoft SQL Server plugin enabled. New Microsoft SQL objects will be discovered within vRealize Operations and will now be automatically monitored by the solution.

As you will have seen, adding applications into the End Point Operations framework is another straightforward task within vRealize Operations.

Viewing your application end points in vRealize Operations

As soon as the application plugin is installed, the related application objects will be automatically discovered in vRealize Operations. Just as they were with the operating system objects, **relationships** between objects will also be created.

Let's take a look at the following:

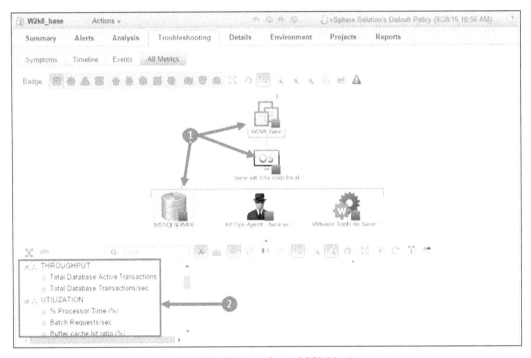

VM/OS/SQL hierarchy and SQL Metrics

1. If we go back to **Troubleshooting | All Metrics**, we can now see that our virtual machine is a **parent** of the Windows operating system and our Windows operating system is now a **parent** of **MSSQLSERVER**.

   The MSSQLSERVER object represents the Microsoft SQL application, as a whole, that has been installed on this host.

2. Clicking on the MSSQLSERVER object changes the metric selector context, and you can see a much wider set of metrics, including the addition of **THROUGHPUT** metrics.

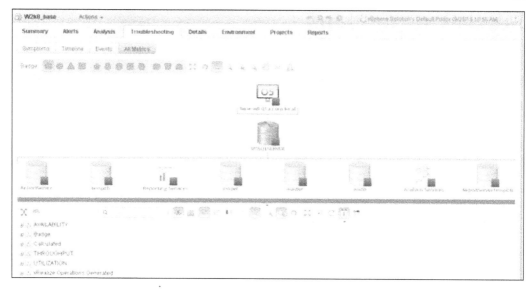

OS and SQL hierarchy

3. Double-clicking on the MSSQLSERVER will change the focus of the relationship tree, and we will see all **Databases** and monitored **SQL services** that are **child** objects of the MSSQLSERVER application.

All the new objects will also be visible in **Environment Overview | Inventory Trees | MSSQL Cluster Instances and Services**, as shown in the following screenshot. Here, you can also see how the hierarchy is represented.

SQL Environment Overview

MS SQL dashboard

When the Solution Pack is installed, it also installs a dashboard for monitoring Microsoft SQL, as shown in the following screenshot:

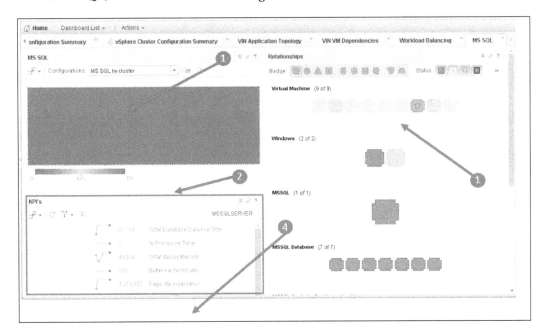

1. The top left has a **Heatmap** representing all the Microsoft SQL servers discovered in your environment. Clicking on an object here sets the context for all the other widgets in the dashboard.

2. The next panel is the **KPI**, or **Key Performance Indicators**, widget. This shows some key metrics for the selected Microsoft SQL server.

3. On the right-hand side is the **Relationships** widget. This shows the relationships of virtual machines, Microsoft SQL servers, and their databases and services. It is contextual to the heatmap, meaning that when an object is selected in the heatmap, all of its related objects are highlighted in the relationship tree.

4. If you scroll down, you can see an **Alerts** widget showing all the open alerts, in vRealize Operations Manager for the selected Microsoft SQL Server.

Policies and End Point Operations

The number of metrics that can be made available by applications can be quite staggering. For example, with Microsoft SQL Solution for vRealize Operations, there are hundreds of metrics available.

 All the metrics for a given Solution Pack are typically listed in the installation documentation—in the case of the Microsoft SQL Solution for vRealize Operations, they take up about half of the 24-page document!

With the quantity of collected metrics being key to the sizing and performance of vRealize Operations, the Solution Pack authors typically only configure a subset of the metrics to be collected, out-of-the-box, by vRealize Operations. This approach also helps with "noise"—sometimes, too much information can be overload and unnecessary.

At times, there will be metrics, however, that you want to monitor which are not being collected. For example, your DBAs may have specific KPIs that they need to maintain, that are determined by a specific set of metrics. In these cases, you may need to enable or disable some of the metrics being collected.

Enabling and disabling of metric collections is carried out by Policies, so let's look at how we can change the collected metrics in vRealize Operations:

 In the following example, we are going to make changes to the Default Policy—this will impact the collection of metrics for all associated objects. If you want to make changes for just a subset of objects, then you can use Groups and assign specific Policies to these groups, as described in *Chapter 2, Install, Configure, and Administer vRealize Operations Manager*.

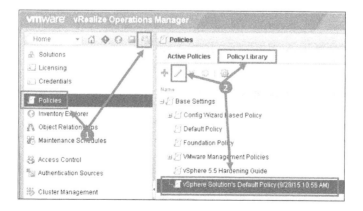

1. To start, we need to open the **Default policy**. To do this, navigate to **Administration | Policies**.

2. Select the **Policy Library** tab, locate and highlight your default policy and click on the *Pencil* icon to edit it.

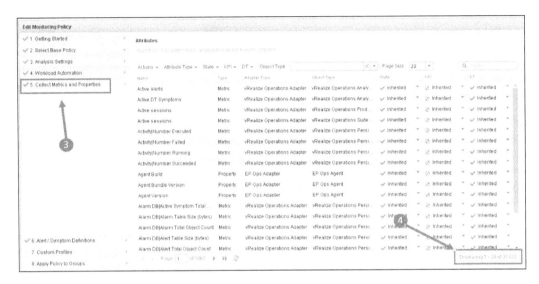

3. Click on **5. Collect Metrics and Properties**.

4. Notice the quantity of metrics and properties. In this lab, I have over 21,000 — we will need to do some **filtering**.

5. The best way to filter, initially, will be by **Object Type**. We probably want to make changes to each impacted object type in turn. For Microsoft SQL Solution for vRealize Operations, eight new object types will have been created:

   ° MSSQL

   ° MSSQL Agent

   ° MSSQL Analysis Services

   ° MSSQL Cluster

   ° MSSQL Database

   ° MSSQL Databases

   ° MSSQL Reporting Services

   ° MSSQL World

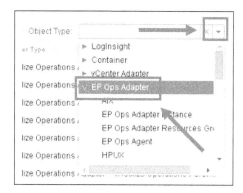

6. Click on the **Object Type** dropdown arrow, and then expand **EP Ops Adapter**. Scroll down until you locate the eight MSSQL object types. Now, select the first object type that you wish to filter on. In the following screenshot, we have filtered by **MSSQL**.

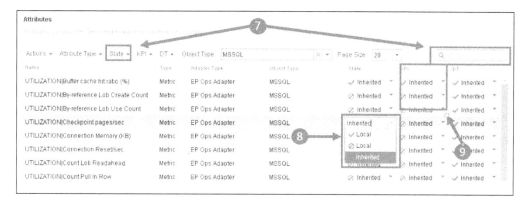

7. You can filter further as required. You may want to use the **State** filter to filter only on metrics that are enabled with a *Tick* sign, or disabled with the *Barred* icon. Alternatively, if you know the name of the metric that you are looking for, you can use the filter text box.

8. Once you find the metric that you are interested in, you can use the dropdown to change its setting to the following:

   ° **Ticked Local**: This means that the metric will be collected by objects with this policy applied.

   ° **Barred Local**: This means that the metric will **not** be collected by objects with this policy applied.

   ° **Inherited**: The metric collection will be determined by the parent policy. The **effective state** will be shown by a *tick* or the *barred* icon.

9. Finally, once you have made all the changes you need to click on **Save** to save the policy.

Summary

In this final chapter, we have looked at how the End Point Operations capability can be added to vRealize Operations, to extend your monitoring and management to operating systems and applications.

We have looked at how the End Point Operations agent is installed and how you can add Solution Packs to monitor applications, such as Microsoft SQL Server.

We then looked at how the new End Point Operations objects are surfaced and used in the vRealize Operations UI. Finally, we looked at how you can use Policy to tune the metrics being collected.

This concludes this *vRealize Operations Manager Essentials* book. We hope that you found it useful and that you are now able to use the solution to great effect in your environment.

Index

Thank you for buying
VMware vRealize Operations Essentials

About Packt Publishing

Packt, pronounced 'packed', published its first book, *Mastering phpMyAdmin for Effective MySQL Management*, in April 2004, and subsequently continued to specialize in publishing highly focused books on specific technologies and solutions.

Our books and publications share the experiences of your fellow IT professionals in adapting and customizing today's systems, applications, and frameworks. Our solution-based books give you the knowledge and power to customize the software and technologies you're using to get the job done. Packt books are more specific and less general than the IT books you have seen in the past. Our unique business model allows us to bring you more focused information, giving you more of what you need to know, and less of what you don't.

Packt is a modern yet unique publishing company that focuses on producing quality, cutting-edge books for communities of developers, administrators, and newbies alike. For more information, please visit our website at www.packtpub.com.

About Packt Enterprise

In 2010, Packt launched two new brands, Packt Enterprise and Packt Open Source, in order to continue its focus on specialization. This book is part of the Packt Enterprise brand, home to books published on enterprise software – software created by major vendors, including (but not limited to) IBM, Microsoft, and Oracle, often for use in other corporations. Its titles will offer information relevant to a range of users of this software, including administrators, developers, architects, and end users.

Writing for Packt

We welcome all inquiries from people who are interested in authoring. Book proposals should be sent to author@packtpub.com. If your book idea is still at an early stage and you would like to discuss it first before writing a formal book proposal, then please contact us; one of our commissioning editors will get in touch with you.

We're not just looking for published authors; if you have strong technical skills but no writing experience, our experienced editors can help you develop a writing career, or simply get some additional reward for your expertise.

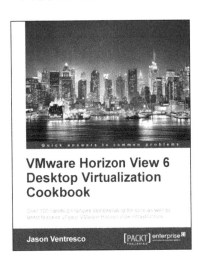

VMware Horizon View 6 Desktop Virtualization Cookbook

ISBN: 978-1-78217-164-5   Paperback: 332 pages

Over 100 hands-on recipes demonstrating the core as well as latest features of your VMware Horizon View infrastructure

1. Gain a detailed insight into the configuration and administration of core features of VMware Horizon View.

2. Learn how to deploy the newest features of the VMware Horizon View 6.0 such as Cloud Pod Architecture, VSAN integration, and more.

3. Benefit from practical examples that provide a greater level of detail than the VMware Horizon View documentation.

VMware ESXi Cookbook

ISBN: 978-1-78217-006-8   Paperback: 334 pages

Over 50 reciepes to master VMware vSphere administration

1. Understand the concepts of virtualization by deploying vSphere web client to perform vSphere administration.

2. Learn important aspects of vSphere including administration, security, performance, and configuring vSphere Management Assistant (VMA) to run commands and scripts without the need to authenticate every attempt.

3. VMware ESXi 5.1 Cookbook is a recipe-based guide to the administration of VMware vSphere.

Please check **www.PacktPub.com** for information on our titles

VMware vCenter Operations Manager Essentials

ISBN: 978-1-78217-696-1   Paperback: 246 pages

Explore virtualization fundamentals and real-world solutions for the modern network administrator

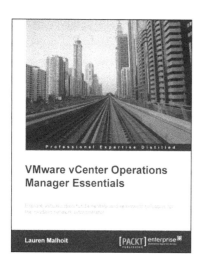

VMware vCenter Operations Manager Essentials

Lauren Malhoit

1. Written by VMware expert Lauren Malhoit, this book takes a look at vCenter Operations Manager from a practical point of view that every administrator can appreciate.

2. Understand, troubleshoot, and design your virtual environment in a better and more efficient way than you ever have before.

3. A step-by-step and learn-by-example guide to understanding the ins and outs of vCenter Operations Manager.

VMware vSphere 5.x Datacenter Design Cookbook

ISBN: 978-1-78217-700-5   Paperback: 260 pages

Over 70 recipes to design a virtual datacenter for performance, availability, manageability, and recoverability with VMware vSpehere 5.x

VMware vSphere 5.x Datacenter Design Cookbook

Hersey Cartwright

1. Innovative recipes, offering numerous practical solutions when designing virtualized datacenters.

2. Identify the design factors—requirements, assumptions, constraints, and risks—by conducting stakeholder interviews and performing technical assessments.

3. Increase and guarantee performance, availability, and workload efficiency with practical steps and design considerations.

Please check **www.PacktPub.com** for information on our titles

www.ingramcontent.com/pod-product-compliance
Lightning Source LLC
Chambersburg PA
CBHW062113050326

40690CB00016B/3294